The Complete Guide to
Washington
Quarters

By
John Feigenbaum

Virginia Beach, Virginia

DLRC Press
6095 Indian River Road, Suite #200
Virginia Beach, Virginia 23464
(804) 424-0560 • fax (804) 424-2363

Printed in the United States

Look for these and other titles from DLRC Press:

The Complete Guide to Buffalo Nickels by David W. Lange

The Complete Guide to Mercury Dimes by David W. Lange

The Complete Guide to Liberty Seated Half Dimes
by Al Blythe

The Complete Guide to Liberty Seated Dimes by Brian Greer

The Complete Guide to Liberty Seated Half Dollars
by Wiley & Bugert

The Complete Guide to Barber Dimes by David Lawrence

The Complete Guide to Barber Quarters by David Lawrence

The Complete Guide to Barber Halves by David Lawrence

The Complete Guide to Walking Liberty Half Dollars
by Bruce Fox

*The Comprehensive Catalog and Encyclopedia of United
States Morgan and Peace Silver Dollars*
(the "VAM" book) by Van Allen & Mallis

Coming soon...

The Complete Guide to Barber Quarters, 2nd Edition
by David Lawrence

The Complete Guide to Franklin & Kennedy Half Dollars

Dedicated to my wonderful
wife, Rachael, who means
everything to me.

Acknowledgements

The date and mint-mark photography was provided by Tom Mulvaney. He is responsible for nearly all the photos without credit lines. Most of the remaining photos, which include a number of the errors and nearly every variety shown were provided by Bill Fivaz and J.T. Stanton whose contribution was invaluable to this book.

A special thanks goes to Charles Kirtley, a specialist in medals and tokens, and J.P. Martin of the American Numismatic Association who provided special sections in their respective fields of expertise and to Elliot Goldman of Allstate Rare Coins for his foreword and valuable comments on certain dates.

I would also like to extend my appreciation to my mother Lynn for providing her professional editing expertise (which, I have to admit, was sorely needed).

The following people were also very helpful and provided the use of their coins and/or very useful information and insight to the preparation of this book: Phil Carrigan, Barbara Gregory, Earl Hawthorne, Bill Kemp, David Lawrence, Robert Lehmann, Harry Miller, Paul Neuenkirk, Fred Weinberg, David Woloch and J.J. Woodside.

Thanks also to the following institutions for providing access and permission to their archives: American Numismatic Association Library and Authentication Bureau and the Smithsonian Institution National Museum of American History.

The following organizations provided permission to reprint information from their publications: Western Publishing Company - *A Guidebook of United States Coins* by R.S. Yoeman; Numismatic Guaranty Corp. - *NGC Census*; CDN, Inc. - *The Coin Dealer Newsletter and Monthly Summary;* Amos Press - *Coin World;* Krause Publications - *Numismatic News;* American Numismatic Association - *The Numismatist*.

Foreword

by Elliot S. Goldman

When you think back of the sets that we all collected as kids, Washington quarters must be included. I remember looking through change back in the 1950's and 1960's, trying to find the elusive 1932-D and -S dates. As I got older and wanted to put an uncirculated set together, most every coin I looked at had unsightly bag marks on Washington's head because of the high relief. It was and still is very difficult to find nice gem coins, and that's the reason for my optimism for this popular series.

Today, the collector or collector/investor can purchase PCGS or NGC certified coins in MS65 to MS67 at unbelievably low prices. MS65 certified coins in the 1930's are genuinely scarce, and can be purchased for $50-$75 each for "P" mints. If you look around the bourse floor of any coin show or check through advertisements in the coin magazines, you'll find that nice pieces are seldom offered. How can something that's widely collected and seldom seen nice be so inexpensive? Original rolls of quarters in the 1930's are not around, which means that few coins will be graded in the future. In addition, it is very likely that prices will increase substantially. Since it costs some $25 to have a coin graded, values will have to increase before some dates are submitted. In other words, it's virtually impossible for this series not to have tremendous potential.

I put together a nice set myself and have recommended to my friends that they do the same. It only makes sense since prices of nice coins are so low. There is almost no down-side risk, and the sky is the limit.

I'm really glad to see that John has put this book together — we in the hobby needed a clear and concise focus on Washington quarters.

Enjoy yourselves and happy hunting!

Elliot S. Goldman
Professional Numismatist
Allstate Coin Co.

Introduction

The Washington quarter series is a great set to put together. In assembling this book, I wanted to provide a reference for all those interested in this series from the casual observer to the advanced collector and the investor.

For the beginner, the Washington quarter series offers a selection of more than 130 coins, all affordable. Prices start at face value and rarely go over a few dollars per coin in circulated grades.

For the advanced collector, it's remarkable to find a series in which most dates are still readily available in flashy uncirculated grades for less than $20 per coin. Yet the set is challenging because of the early dates.

The investor also has strong incentive to buy Washington quarters. Many dates sell for a fraction of the prices they commanded in 1991 — and they were arguably undervalued then.

It has truly been a pleasure compiling this book and I hope you will find it useful. Comments are welcome, especially regarding new variety discoveries.

John Feigenbaum
March 1994

Please contact me at:
c/o David Lawrence Rare Coins
P.O. Box 64844
Virginia Beach, VA 23467

Table of Contents

Chapter 1

HISTORY OF THE SERIES
&
MAJOR DESIGN CHANGES

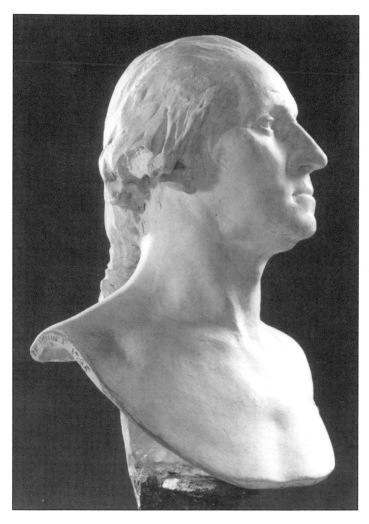

George Washington (1732-1799), sculpted into clay form by Jean Antoine Houdon in 1785. The Washington family regarded the Houdon bust as the best likeness of the first President. The bust is on permanent display in the museum at Mount Vernon, Virginia.

(Courtesy of Mt. Vernon Ladies' Association)

John Feigenbaum

History of the Series

The Washington quarter that has been a staple of our economy for more than six decades had a contentious start mired in power plays and male chauvinism. Yet it began as a worthy endeavor. The inspiration behind the quarter was a 1931 Treasury Department proposal to commemorate the bicentennial anniversary of our founding father's birth in 1732 by putting Washington's likeness on a new coin. Originally the coin was going to be a half dollar but the denomination was subsequently changed to a quarter dollar by Congress.

As was common practice at the time, a design competition was held. Artists were invited to submit their designs (in plaster model form) to a committee co-sponsored by the Treasury Department and the Washington Bicentennial Commission with cooperation from the national Commission of Fine Arts. The winning design would be used for the new quarter as well as for a special-issue congressional medal (see *The Many Medals Depicting George Washington*, page 14). The only restrictions were that the obverse had to be based on Houdon's bust of Washington and the reverse had to depict a national symbol (e.g. a bald eagle or shield).

The committee unanimously selected the model designed by sculptor Laura Gardin Fraser. The wife of sculptor James Earle Fraser (of Buffalo nickel fame), Laura Fraser, was highly regarded. She is best known for her design of the Oregon Trail commemorative coins minted from 1926 through 1939.

Unfortunately, the final decision fell to Secretary of the Treasury Andrew W. Mellon. The stubborn Mellon refused to approve the Fraser design on the basis that he had not been party to the agreement.[1] Mellon requested a second competition in which he could take a more active role. On October 27, 1931, the joint committee selected six choices from more than 100 models, again picking Laura Fraser's model (labeled #56) as its first choice. On November 2, Mellon reviewed the committee's choices and had this to say in a memorandum to Charles Moore, chairman of the Commission of Fine Arts (dated Nov. 4):

Laura Gardin Fraser submitted these models as her entry (#56) for the Washington head quarter. They were unanimously recommended by the Commission of Fine Arts and the Washington Bicentennial Commission in 1931 but rejected by the secretary of the Treasury.

John Feigenbaum

Following the conference we had with the members of the Fine Arts Commission two days ago, I inspected the models of the design for the new quarter dollar selected by the Commission as the one most nearly meeting their approval. I understand that you wish the sculptor given an opportunity to restudy this design in order to make certain changes which would meet with my own and your wishes in the matter.

I am very glad to accede to your request for a restudy of the design but, as the one selected was not my first choice and as it might be construed as showing discrimination if we give this opportunity to one sculptor and not extend it to others whose designs have equal merits in my eyes, I have designated the designs of three other sculptors and shall be glad to have a restudy made by these sculptors and by the one designated by the Commission...

Walter Breen, in his "Complete Encyclopedia of U.S. and Colonial Coins," notes that "it has been learned that Mellon knew all along who submitted the winning models, and his male chauvinism partly or wholly motivated his unwillingness to let a woman win."[2]

After the rebuke by Mellon, Moore once again reaffirmed the Commission's position on the Fraser model in his November 10 reply to the Treasury secretary:

The Commission feel that this design would result in a very excellent coin. They quite agree with the Secretary's criticism that the eagle should be strengthened by a more vigorous treatment of head and body and a modification of the movement of the wings.

From the point of general design this model seems to the Commission easily the best of the four under consideration. Therefore, they respectfully advise that it be accepted and that the sculptor be required to modify his existing model in the particulars stated above.[3]

In yet another attempt to convince the Secretary, Moore wrote on January 20:

In accordance with your request, the Commission of Fine Arts on January 19, 1932, considered the models selected from the number submitted in the original competition for re-study and re-submission.

The Commission selected from among the models an obverse and reverse which they marked. These selected models in the judgment of the Commission, adequately and in a distinguished manner meet what the Commission believe to be requirements for the design of the most used and so most representative coin of the United States. The models were numbered 56...

Moore's letter went on to criticize the design Mellon favored, (entered by John Flanagan):

The Commission considered the alternative designs submitted by the above artist [Fraser] recommended to you as in a class by themselves. Which of the alternatives is the best was the question.... This decision was based on a combination of elements in the design which seemed to the Commission to be the most artistic one...

...The Commission, however, found in a design which called for detailed examination a lack of simplicity and vigor in the head, and an artistically unfortunate and also an unnatural arrangement of the hair which became inconspicuous in the reduced size representing the actual coin. The reverse was pictorial rather than medallic in character. For these reasons the Commission felt that the design lacked these very elements of universality and permanence which the quarter-dollar should embody.

The Commission also considered a suggestion that the Saint-Gaudens eagle on the twenty-dollar gold piece be used for the reverse. They considered that to use a design that had been used on another coin would be unfortunate and sure to provoke criticism. Moreover, the eagle as it now appears on the coin has lost that essential quality which Saint-Gaudens gave to it. In reducing the relief vigor has been lost. Now the eagle has the quality of an engraving: It has become a picture instead of an emblem.

In submitting for your consideration advice as to the selec-

　　　　　　　　　　　　　　　　　John Feigenbaum

tion of designs for the new quarter-dollar, the Commission have been guided by the experience of its members in the art of the medal also with the art of coinage. They have given to this particular recommendation most careful consideration, based on such experience. Also they have felt the responsibility laid upon them both toward the Government which they serve and to the Fine Arts which they are appointed to represent".[4]

A few weeks later, Mellon was succeeded by Ogden L. Mills and Moore restated his argument for model #56 in a last-ditch attempt to sway the new Treasury secretary. Mills, however, was not one to alter the motions put forth by the former incumbent and on April 11, he had this reply for Moore:

...My predecessor in office, Honorable A.W. Mellon, gave thought and attention to the models submitted in the competition and finally selected the particular model in question. In light of your suggestions, I gave further thought to the matter and certain changes have been made by the artist, prompted by these considerations. I have given further consideration to the subject and am constrained to adhere to the decision of my predecessor, and I selected that model.

You will realize, of course, that the duty of making the selection falls upon the Secretary of the Treasury and not upon the Commission of Fine Arts, the function of that body being purely advisory."[5]

The matter was finally put to rest on April 16, 1932 when Secretary Mills formally named the model designed by John Flanagan as the design for the next United States quarter dollar.

John Flanagan
(1895-1952)

The artist responsible for the design of the Washington quarter was born on April 7, 1895 in North Dakota where he spent most of his early years in an orphanage. A passion for drawing, wood carving and painting led him to the Minneapolis Institute of Arts in 1914 where he studied for three years until the outset of World War I.

After serving in the United States Merchant Marine from 1917 through 1922, he lived in New York City where he was befriended by painter Arthur B. Davies. Flanagan eventually spent time on Davies' farm in Congers, New York to recuperate from deteriorating health. As his rehabilitation progressed so did his artistic abilities.

Flanagan continued painting and expanded his talents to sculpting, which he practiced exclusively by 1928. His designs ranged from small animals to works bearing mother-and-child, a theme that was most recurrent in his repertoire. In 1931, his plaster model contest entry was ultimately selected by the secretary of the Treasury Andrew W. Mellon over 100 other entries as the final design of the Washington head quarter.

In 1934, Flanagan suffered a nervous breakdown and a tragic automobile accident five years later forced him to quit his stone sculpting altogether. His health, both mental and physical, began to decline and he committed suicide at the age of 56 on January 6, 1952.[6,7]

Authors note: Not much is known about John Flanagan. Unfortunately the two primary sources I was able to find offered two different dates of birth and death. I decided to use the "Venus Numismatics Dictionary" as my primary source because it contained a little more detail than the "Catalog of Coin Designs and Designers."

Major Design Changes

Once a model has been approved for use in new coinage, the Mint takes over and produces "hubs" from which the actual coining dies are prepared. This process ensures a consistency in all the dies of a given period. If the Mint discovers a defect in the coins (such as uneven wear or stacking problems), the hub can be touched up and new dies prepared from that single source and the problem corrected. Hub changes are not to be confused with alterations to a specific "die" which result in what collectors refer to as "errors." These errors, produced while the die is being prepared, account for only a small percentage of a given mintage.

"Light Motto": 1932-1934 (Type I)

When Secretary of the Treasury Ogden Mills finally approved Flanagan's design for the new quarter on April 16, everyone from the Bicentennial Commission to local banks to the general public was clamoring for the new coins, especially as no coins had been minted the previous year. This forced the Mint to hasten preparation of the hubs, which were used from 1932-1934. The dies produced from the original hubs are characterized by a severe weakness in the obverse motto and in Washington's hair. This finding further validates the Commission of Fine Arts' initial criticism of the design at the time. The Commission felt that when the models were reduced "to the actual size of the coin, some details now visible would be lost…"[8]

- Used exclusively in 1932, and in 1934 at the Philadelphia Mint only until it was replaced by the Type II & III hubs later that year.
- Characterized by a weak or blurred motto.

"Medium Motto": 1934-1935   (Type II)
- Used in 1934 along with Type I & III hubs and exclusively in 1935.

"Heavy Motto": 1934-1964   (TYPE III)
- Used in 1934 along with Type I & II hubs and exclusively from 1935 to 1964. Most easily identified by middle point of "W" in "WE" which is higher than outer strokes of the letter.

Light or "weak" motto: 1932-1934

Medium motto: 1934-1935

Heavy motto: 1934, 1936-1964

Table 1-1 on page 11 shows which motto types were hubbed by the various mints during the years they were used.

From 1936 through 1964 a number of small changes were made to the obverse design. In 1938 and 1944, for example, the outline of Washington's profile was sharpened. Anyone who takes the time to carefully examine the designs from year to year will be duly rewarded and discover many minor modifications. This constant retouching of the master hubs and dies is clear evidence that the mint engravers have never been truly satisfied with their final product.

Table 1-1: Motto Varieties on Washington Quarters from 1932-1964

Year-Mint	— MOTTO —		
	Light	Medium	Heavy
1932-P	X		
1932-D	X		
1932-S	X		
1934-P	X	X	X
1934-D		X	X
1935-P		X	
1935-D		X	
1935-S		X	
1936-1964 (all mints)			X

There are three distinct reverse hubs in the series as follows:

Reverse Hub A: 1932-1964
- ES of STATES nearly touch.
- Leaf extends to the height of top-most arrowpoint.
- Leaf above first L in DOLLAR is very weak at the tip and does not touch.
- Leaf above A in DOLLAR extremely weak and may not show at all.

Reverse Hub B: 1936-1972
  Used on all proofs from 1936-1972 and inconsistently on business strikes from 1956 through 1972.
- ES of STATES apart.
- Leaf extends above the top-most arrowpoint.
- Leaves above first L and A in DOLLAR clearly make contact.

Reverse Hub C: 1964-1974, 1977-present

Found on most of the business strikes from 1965 through present, although a small number of "transitional" pieces have been discovered dated 1964 with the B reverse. They are extremely rare.

- ES of STATES apart.
- Leaf extends to the height of top-most arrowpoint.
- Leaf above first L in DOLLAR nearly touches.
- Leaf above A in DOLLAR very close and may touch.

Reverse Hub A: 1932-1964

Reverse Hub B: 1936-1972

Reverse Hub C: 1964-1974, 1977-present

The Bicentennial Quarter: 1976

For a single mintage year, the design of the Washington quarter (along with the Kennedy half dollar and the Eisenhower dollar) was changed in commemoration of the Bicentennial celebration of America's Declaration of Independence. The only modification to the obverse was the date, which read: "1776-1976." The entire reverse was redesigned by Jack Ahr. These coins were struck in silver-clad (for special mint and proof sets) and nickel-clad for regular issue. No quarters were minted in 1976 without the Bicentennial modifications (also see 1976 quarter, Chapter 4).

To commemorate our nation's bicentennial anniversary, the Senate authorized a one-year commemorative reverse design for the Washington quarter. Note the date on the obverse was changed to read: "1776-1976".

The Many Medals Depicting George Washington

By Charles E. Kirtley

No figure or subject in American history has been commemorated in medallic art more than George Washington. Starting while he was still in office, the first President has been portrayed on coins, tokens, medals, plaques, patterns and badges.

The earliest medallic portraits of Washington are found on our early coinage. There is an extensive list of early coppers portraying Washington, which were struck mainly in Great Britain. Some of the more familiar early issues include the Washington series of Colonial coinage, some early pattern coins issued by Robert Birch and early medals commemorating events in the Revolution. The most famous of these is the "Washington Before Boston" medal which was struck in France in 1786 (pictured below). The obverse shows a bust of Washington and his soldiers as they prepared to retake Boston from the British during the Revolutionary War. A gold specimen was presented to Washington himself and now resides in the Boston Historical Society. So popular was this medal that it was re-struck many times, and a version is still being made for collectors at the U.S. Mint.

The popular "Washington Before Boston" medal, originally struck in France in 1786, is still being produced today by the U.S. Mint. Actual size: 68mm in diameter. (Courtesy Charles Kirtley)

Washington's death in 1799 sparked an outpouring of medallic tributes to his life and to commemorate the nation's loss. The most important of the medals at this time were the funeral medals issued in 1799 and 1800 when his passing was publicly mourned in Boston funeral processions. The 1799 procession was commemorated by a funeral medal with a skull and crossbones on its reverse. This type was worn by the Masons who participated in the parade. The second type has a funeral urn on its reverse and was worn in the public parade in 1800. Both types depict Washington's bust facing left within a wreath. The legend: "HE IS IN GLORY, THE WORLD IN TEARS." encircles the wreath.

Following the Colonial period, Washington was often seen on trade tokens, his bust on one side and a merchant's advertisement on the other. These medallic emissions were most numerous during the Civil War when literally hundreds of different tokens were made bearing a likeness of Washington.

During the Centennial of our country in 1876 there was a large outpouring of medallic issues commemorating events surrounding the birth of our country. George Washington is prominent in this series. One of the more popular issues is a medal showing him refusing to be crowned king.

Another event that precipitated many Washington medallic portraits was the centennial of his inauguration in 1889. Some of the more interesting issues include a famous portrait of Washington by Augustus St. Gaudens, designer of the $20 gold piece minted from 1907-1933.

The 20th century saw Washington's popularity remain high in medallic tributes. Many commemoratives were issued by numismatists like Max Schwartz, Stack's, Thomas Elder and by *Numismatic News*. Others were made by merchants who used Washington's likeness on the advertising tokens.

In 1932 a large number of medals and store cards were issued at the 150th anniversary of the first inauguration. The U.S. Mint also produced a medal in conjunction with its release of the new Washington quarter. This date also coincided with the New York World's Fair and with the Golden Gate International Exposition. Both events served as venues for large numbers of Washington material to be issued and distributed.

Most recently, large quantities of Washingtonia issues occurred during the U.S Bicentennial commemoration in 1976, with private mints, governments and others issuing coins, medals and bars depicting the first president.

The 1932 celebration was sanctioned and sponsored by the U.S. government. Other officially-sponsored issues include the U.S. Mint medal designed by Laura Gardin Fraser, who had also been a leading contender in the design for the quarter.

Medallic portraits of Washington are still being turned out today. Many private mints have issued medals depicting Washington, events in his life, and historic events in which he played a part. In the field of token and medal collecting, Washingtonia remains one of the most avidly sought after subjects.

For further reading on this subject, see "Medallic Portraits of Washington," by Russell Rulau.

Charles E. Kirtley is an authority on American medals, tokens and related items. He operates a retail/mail-bid operation in Elizabeth City, North Carolina.

This medal, designed by Laura Gardin Fraser, was minted and distributed in 1932 in conjunction with the release of the new Washington quarter. Actual size is 56mm in diameter. (Courtesy Charles Kirtley)

John Feigenbaum

Chapter 2

ALTERED AND COUNTERFEIT COINS
&
GALLERY OF ERRORS

Altered & Counterfeit Coins

By J.P. Martin, ANA Numismatist

The Washington quarter series is plagued by an alarmingly high number of counterfeits, some with a sophistication not seen in other series of United States coins. If there is any question as to the authenticity of a 1932-D, 1932-S, 1934-D or 1936-D the reader is urged to send the coin to the American Numismatic Association Authentication Bureau (ANAAB) for a professional opinion. (Certification by one of the major services – PCGS, NGC, ANACS – also guarantees authenticity.)

The Washington quarter series is plagued by two deceptive struck counterfeits and several "added mintmark" alterations.

The most common added mintmarks are found on the 1932-D, 1932-S, 1934-D and 1936-D quarters. The 1932's are altered far more commonly than the others. They began showing up in quantity in the 1960's and throughout the 1970's. They are, in all likelihood, being produced today, but with more sophistication and in smaller quantities than we have seen in the past.

Since a fairly large quantity of dies were used for the production of these coins, we do not use die polish, mintmark position or other die markers in authentication. [*Editor's note: ANAAB and other authenticators will often look for key diagnostic features on a coin to determine authenticity. For example, a genuine example of a three-legged buffalo nickel will show a distinct raised ridge between the legs of the bison. While the Washington quarters offer a few such references, none are considered conclusive evidence – which makes them very difficult to authenticate.*]

Genuine coins tend to display a crisp, high relief mintmark with distinct serifs that often sit within a slight depression. The mintmark's sharp edges and high relief tend to contrast with the gently rising design features, such as the stems and lettering around it. This led one of my mentors, John Hunter of 1970's ANACS (American Numismatic Association Certification Service) fame, to state, "If it looks good, it's probably bad. And if it looks bad, it's probably good!"

Also due to the high relief of the mintmarks, they often display machine doubling, whereas the design features seldom show any. I have never seen an added mintmark which displayed machine doubling or double punching. Often mintmarks are filled, with no inner openings. This is more characteristic of genuine coins than alterations.

As with any added mintmark, look for evidence of a seam, or tooling and smoothing. Often when adhesive is a solder, you will notice a heat-induced discoloration of the mintmark. After time, solder will oxidize and discolor differently than the surrounding silver. Look for green or white discolorations surrounding the mintmark.

If the adhesive is a glue, if can often be dissolved with a solvent, such as Dissolve™ or acetone.

After some experience, you will develop a "feel" for the "look" of genuine mintmarks.

The accompanying photographs illustrate several examples of genuine and added mintmarks for reference.

For further information, contact:

American Numismatic Association Authentication Bureau
818 North Cascade Avenue
Colorado Springs, CO 80903-3279
719/632-2646

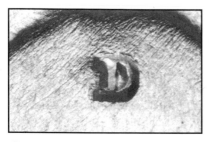

Genuine 1932-D mintmark. Note the distinct serifs and die polishing under the mintmark. The mintmark also sits in a slight depression. (Photo courtesy ANAAB)

This mintmark has been added to a 1932-P. Note the low relief and lack of distinct serifs. (ANAAB)

Genuine 1932-S mintmark which has been set in atop heavy die polishing. (ANAAB)

Another genuine 1932-S mintmark. (ANAAB)

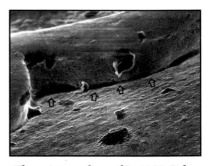

Genuine 1932-D mintmark shown at 300X magnification. The continuous flow lines and lack of seam are proof of this mintmark's authenticity. (ANAAB)

The mintmark on this 1932-D has obviously been added. Note the seam of the coin and the mintmark as shown here at 300X magnification. (ANAAB)

Surprisingly, even some Philadelphia-mint quarters have been counterfeited in quantity. The 1932-P and 1934-P quarters initially seem unlikely targets for a counterfeiter, as they are fairly common. However, when they were discovered in 1984, rolls of these coins were trading at over $2,000 each. They were produced in large quantities, with minimal bag marks and displayed proof-like fields. The look was so foreign to 1930's quarters that one dealer remarked, "They are 1930's coins from 1980's dies."

These two dates are probably from the same shop that produced many of the counterfeit 1917 Type 1 quarters. These three coins have the distinction of being the only deceptively struck, counterfeit quarters dated in the twentieth century.

The photos below show diagnostic features of these struck counterfeits.

1934-P counterfeit. Note the raised die tooling under L in LIB-ERTY. (ANAAB)

1934-P counterfeit. Note tooling lines on B in LIBERTY. (ANAAB)

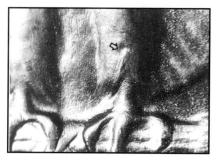

Commonly seen on the counterfeit 1932-P and 1934-P specimens is this die depression on the eagle's left leg (viewer's right). (ANAAB)

The following two coins are examples of crude counterfeit Washington quarters. They are dated 1935 and 1973. Clearly these and others examined were produced for day-to-day use on the street. These counterfeits are easy to detect as the details are often inexact and the surfaces rough. The 1935 specimen is of relatively high quality yet upon examination you will find die lumps and other inconsistencies not found on the genuine article.

1935 counterfeit. Note the raised die lump on the eagle's right (viewer's left) wing. The entire surface is also rough under close examination. (Coin courtesy Harry Miller)

1973 counterfeit. This coin is obviously a crude counterfeit. There are stress cracks all over and the details are very rough and inexact. (Harry Miller)

John Feigenbaum

Gallery of Errors

Even under the strictest standards of quality control, any coin with a mintage in the millions is inevitably going to see a fair number of errors enter the marketplace. The Washington quarter series is no exception. The following coins represent just a few of the errors seen in this series. Rarity ranges from the relatively common (for an off-centered specimen) to the rare (for a coin that has been triple-struck).

Off-center piece dated 1966.
(Courtesy Fred Weinberg)

Undated quarter struck on a dime planchet. (Fred Weinberg)

Undated proof quarter struck with two planchets between the dies.
Somewhere, there's another coin with no reverse.
(Coin courtesy David Woloch)

Undated quarter struck on a clad shell.
(Photo courtesy Bill Fivaz)

1976-D Bicentennial quarter struck off-center with two major clips.
(Bill Fivaz)

Undated Washington quarter, quadruple struck – all off-center.
Very unusual. (Bill Fivaz)

John Feigenbaum

Another unusual coin… this Bicentennial quarter was struck over a previously struck 1976 dime; a so-called "double denomination coin."
(Bill Fivaz)

1980-D struck with a copper streak embedded in the planchet.
(Bill Fivaz)

Undated quarter with a major indentation. Some object must have interfered with the strike.
(Bill Fivaz)

A quarter with a large rim cud at the date. This error is caused by a progressive die crack which eventually leads to a piece of the die falling off. In production, the coin is filled in with extra metal. (Bill Fivaz)

Chapter 3

GRADING

Washington quarters are very difficult to grade in poor states of preservation because obverse detail is often very weak even in mint state. Currently, only a few of the dates in the series are expensive in mint state. For this reason, few of the Washington quarter dates are collected in grades below XF.

Described below are the grading criteria used in the marketplace. Coins do not wear in discrete steps, but gradually. There really are not just a few grades but actually an infinite number of states of wear. Dealers and collectors typically use several grades for describing circulated coins and these are discussed below. Mint state coins have no wear and are judged by a different set of criteria (i.e. the number marks, light hairlines, "freshness", etc.).

Circulated Washington quarters are almost exclusively graded by the obverse detail. This is due to the characteristics of the design and the protection afforded by the rim. In addition, coins from 1932 and 1934 (light motto) cannot be graded by motto detail as the words IN GOD WE TRUST were often faint to begin with.

About Good (AG)

The rim will be worn considerably into the letters and the date.

Good-Very Good (G-VG)

The rim will be worn just in to the tops of the letters and bottom of the date. Coins that grade Very Good exhibit slightly more central detail than coins grading Good. (It is difficult to distinguish between these two grade in Washington quarters.)

Fine (F)

OBVERSE: There will be a full rim. Washington's hairline will begin to show at his forehead. The rest of the hair should also show slight detail.

REVERSE: There will usually be a full rim. Feathers may show on the eagle's breast.

Very Fine (VF)

OBVERSE: Washington's hairline above the forehead begins to show three-dimensionality. The rest of the hair should show detail as well.

REVERSE: The reverse is not generally used to determine this grade, unless it shows an unusual degree of wear or damage.

Extremely Fine (XF)

OBVERSE: All the hair on Washington's head shows detail. The locks of hair at the neck begin to show separation.

REVERSE: The reverse is not generally used to determine this grade, unless it shows an unusual degree of wear or damage.

About Uncirculated (AU)

OBVERSE: This coin exhibits only a trace of wear at its high points: the top of the forehead, Washington's cheek and the lock of hair behind his ear will be slightly flat. Coins should have mint luster.

REVERSE: Only a trace of wear will be visible on the eagle's chest; however breast feathers may be weak due to strike.

Uncirculated (MS60-MS70)

It is difficult and beyond the scope of this book to describe the subtle differences between the various uncirculated grades. Uncirculated coins, by definition, have never been exposed to daily use or circulation, even for a short period of time. Most often, the obverse of the coin holds the telltale clues of a coin's grade. This is because the reverse of most coins grades higher than the obverse.

To achieve the minimum standard of being uncirculated (grading MS60) the coin must exhibit no wear even at its highest points. It can, however, show evidence of mishandling such as bag marks, hairlines, and so on. Professionals will often first examine Washington's high cheek bone (just under the eye) for signs of "rub" which is usually manifested as a break in the luster.

Also examined are the fields in front of and behind Washington's head. The degree to which the fields are hairlined (very light, thin lines noticeable only by rotating the coin carefully under a light) often establishes the "low end" mint-state grade. For example, a coin with many hairlines may be graded AU58. To achieve a grade of MS63 or higher the fields generally must be hairline-free.

The theoretical MS70 coin is absolutely perfect in every way. The coin must be completely devoid of marks or hairlines under 10X magnification, exhibit supreme mint luster and be otherwise flawless to the grader. This grade, almost never achieved, is used as a benchmark. Even a coin fresh from the mint press is likely to exhibit some minor flaw that will keep it from perfection. To date no Washington quarter has been graded higher than MS68 by a major grading service.

(For further assistance in grading mint state coins, the American Numismatic Association sponsors grading seminars that are very helpful. The A.N.A. can be contacted at: 818 North Cascade, Colorado Springs, CO 80903.)

Chapter 4

DATE
&
MINTMARK ANALYSIS

Notes on Chapter 4

1. The values listed under 1949, 1964, 1979 and 1994 are from the 3rd, 17th, 32nd and 47th editions of "A Guide Book of United States Coins" (also referred to as the *Redbook*), a popular retail price guide. CDN values are bid (wholesale) figures from the November 1993 issue of the *Coin Dealer Newsletter Monthly Supplement* and January 28, 1994 issue of the *Coin Dealer Newsletter*.

2. Breen numbers listed are from "Walter Breen's Complete Encyclopedia of U.S. and Colonial Coins."

3. FS numbers listed are from Bill Fivaz and J.T. Stanton's "The Cherrypicker's Guide to Rare Die Varieties," third edition.

4. Total MS/Proof PCGS/NGC refers to the total number of mint state/proof coins listed in the October 1993 *PCGS Population Report* and July 31, 1993 *NGC Census*.

THE SILVER COINAGE
1932-1964

1932

Mintage
Business strikes: 5,404,000

PCGS & NGC Combined Certified Populations

	MS60-62	MS63	MS64	MS65	MS66	MS67
MS	46	203	431	187	19	2

Value

	1949	1964	1979	1994	CDN
VG	—	—	1.75	3.00	2.00
F	—	1.25	2.00	4.00	2.25
VF	—	—	—	6.00	3.25
XF	—	2.25	5.00	9.00	6.00
MS60	1.75	7.00	33.00	—	17.00
MS63	—	—	—	36.00	22.00
MS65	—	—	—	245.00	140.00

Comments
Found with weak motto obverse (see photo below – also Chapter 1, *Major Design Changes*).

The 1932-P is readily available in all grades including mint state. The first year of any issue is generally hoarded by collectors, often in the form of uncirculated rolls and even by the bag. It is very likely that these mini-hoards exist intact, so the certified populations may be artificially low. Nonetheless, fewer Washington quarters were minted in 1932 than in any other year. This is most likely due to the lack of demand as a result of the hard-hitting depression. No coins were minted in 1931 or 1933.

Investors should be wary of the current low population tallies in mint state. The low value of coins grading less than MS65 is a deterrent to submitting these, and a great many uncertified mint state coins probably exist. Elliot Goldman believes, however, that the 1932-P is the toughest coin in the set to find "blazing" white. In MS65 (or higher) this date is in great demand and worth a premium. Most specimens, he adds, are found with unattractive toning.

The 1932-P provides the collector with an excellent opportunity to obtain the first year of issue in mint state at an affordable price. As long as MS64's remain under $50, they're a bargain.

1932-D

Mintage
Business strikes: 436,800

PCGS & NGC Combined Certified Populations

	MS60-62	MS63	MS64	MS65	MS66	MS67
MS	212	214	126	19	0	0

Value

	1949	1964	1979	1994	CDN
VG	—	14.00	45.00	38.00	30.00
F	—	21.00	55.00	50.00	35.00
VF	—	—	—	70.00	45.00
XF	—	55.00	95.00	135.00	105.00
MS60	37.50	150.00	650.00	—	310.00
MS63	—	—	—	775.00	675.00
MS65	—	—	—	4,500.00	3,980.00

Comments
Found with weak motto obverse (see Chapter 1, *Major Design Changes*).

1932-D Continued

The 1932-D is the toughest regular-issue date in the entire series in all grades from Good through Gem. The Denver Mint had not produced quarters since 1929 (and wouldn't again until 1934). The mintage of 436 thousand coins is second lowest in the series — only to the 1932-S. These coins are most commonly found in AG and Good condition which suggests that the majority of the mintage was immediately put into circulation and ignored by the collecting public.

The combined population of PCGS and NGC coins in mint state is 571 coins, compared to 926 for the 1932-S. This trend is magnified as the grade gets higher. No MS66's have been graded as of this writing — a significant fact considering this coin was minted only 62 years ago! The investor should be aware that some "mini-hoards" — perhaps partial rolls — may still exist which have not yet been submitted for grading. Robert Lehmann, a dealer who has dealt in a number of high-end Washington quarters, suggests that the 1932-D is about 5 times tougher to obtain in MS65 than the 1932-S and "you can throw the [CDN] sheet away" as far as pricing is concerned.

Be very careful of altered coins. Due the ready availability of P-mint coins, the 1932-D and -S quarters have become two of the most popular coins of counterfeiters. Chapter 2 details how to detect altered specimens of this date. Use this information as a guide only. Your best protection is certification by one of the major grading services (i.e. PCGS, NGC or ANACS) or authentication by the American Numismatic Association Authentication Bureau (ANAAB). All mint state grades should be certified.

1932-S

Mintage
Business strikes: 408,000

PCGS & NGC Combined Certified Populations

	MS60-62	MS63	MS64	MS65	MS66	MS67
MS	217	333	323	50	3	0

Value

	1949	1964	1979	1994	CDN
VG	—	11.00	42.50	32.00	26.00
F	—	15.00	50.00	37.00	30.00
VF	—	—	—	45.00	35.00
XF	—	25.00	70.00	60.00	42.00
MS60	22.50	60.00	250.00	—	200.00
MS63	—	—	—	450.00	370.00
MS65	—	—	—	3,500.00	2,400.00

Comments
Found with weak motto obverse (see Chapter 1, *Major Design Changes*).

The 1932-S boasts the lowest mintage in the entire regular-issue series and has a desirability second only to the 1932-D. Like its partner minted in Denver, these coin were immediately circulated and, as a result, are most readily found in low grade (AG and Good).

Despite its lower mintage, 1932-S quarters were more aggressively saved in mint state than their Denver counterparts which is evident from the certified population figures. Nearly twice as many (926 versus 571) uncirculated coins have been graded by PCGS and NGC than the 1932-D. In grades MS63 through MS65 the population is double, and nearly triple, the 1932-D. Like the other coins in the 1932 series, flashy white specimens in high grade are prohibitively difficult to find and worth a premium.

Be very careful of altered coins. Due the ready availability of P-mint coins, the 1932-D and -S quarters have become two of the most popular coins of counterfeiters. Chapter 2 details how to detect altered specimens of this date. Use this information as a guide only. Your best protection is certification by one of the major grading services (i.e. PCGS, NGC or ANACS) or authentication by the American Numismatic Association Authentication Bureau (ANAAB). All mint state grades should be certified.

1934

Mintage
Business strikes (All types): 31,912,052

Varieties
Refer to Chapter 1, "Major Design Changes" for a full discussion and photos of the various motto types.

101   Light motto. Mintage estimate: 500,000 (Breen-4270) *(photo)*

102   Medium motto. Mintage estimate: 28,000,000 (Breen-4271)

102a   Doubled die obverse (DDO), medium motto. Mintage unknown, but believed to be very low. (Breen-4272, FS#25¢-009) *(photo)*

103   Heavy motto. Mintage estimate: 3,400,000 (Breen-4273)

PCGS & NGC Combined Certified Populations

	MS60-62	MS63	MS64	MS65	MS66	MS67
101	3	9	18	32	5	0
102a	3	9	7	3	0	0
102, 103	26	100	396	373	95	7

Value for 102, 103

	1949	1964	1979	1994	CDN
VG	—	—	1.75	1.75	—
F	—	1.25	2.00	2.50	1.25
VF	—	—	—	4.00	1.75
XF	—	2.90	4.00	6.00	2.50
MS60	2.75	10.00	18.00	—	15.00
MS63	—	—	—	31.00	18.00
MS65	—	—	—	125.00	60.00

Comments

The 1934-P claims the distinction of being the only coin minted with all three motto types: light, medium and heavy. While none of these varieties are currently priced at any real premium, the shrewd collector would be wise to look for light motto (101) specimens, as they are in very short supply. The bulk of these are found circulated and are much tougher in mint state grades than the medium or heavy motto types. Light motto specimens currently trade at a premium. However, as demand and popularity for this variety increase, so will the price. Elliot Goldman of Allstate Rare Coins regularly sells light motto specimens for about four times the price of medium or heavy motto coins. PCGS and NGC both distinguish between the light motto and "normal" mottos (a combination of the medium and heavy motto types).

The doubled die obverse (102a) is a far more popular variety than the varying motto weights and is quite often sought by those who wish to collect the entire set (and can afford one). The 1994 *Redbook* lists the value of these from $75 in VF to $1,500 in MS65. According to *The Cherrypickers Guide to Rare Die Varieties*, "this variety can still be found, mostly in circulated condition." They represent an excellent value at these prices and could prove to be a wise investment. Double die coins have always been desirable. However, be aware that these premiums are for coins which exhibit a strong doubling on the obverse motto. Weaker die states are worth considerably less and have far less potential.

After the hiatus of 1933, the Mint stepped up production and minted nearly 32 million quarters in Philadelphia this year. While some original rolls surely remain intact, uncirculated specimens are still a bargain at today's levels.

Light motto

101. 1934 Doubled die obverse.
(Photo courtesy of J.T. Stanton –
Cherrypickers' Guide)

1934-D

Mintage
Business strikes: 3,527,200

Varieties
Refer to Chapter 1, "Major Design Changes" for a full discussion and photos of the various motto types.

101 Medium motto. Mintage estimate: 1,000,000 (Breen-4274) *(photo)*

101a D/D, Medium motto. (Breen-4275)

102 Heavy motto. Mintage estimate: 2,500,000 (Breen-4276) *(photo)*

PCGS & NGC Combined Certified Populations

	MS60-62	MS63	MS64	MS65	MS66	MS67
MS	36	99	174	81	10	0

Value

	1949	1964	1979	1994	CDN
VG	—	—	2.25	3.00	3.50
F	—	2.50	5.00	4.00	3.75
VF	—	—	—	8.00	5.00
XF	—	7.50	15.00	11.00	9.00
MS60	2.50	42.50	120.00	—	70.00
MS63	—	—	—	75.00	100.00
MS65	—	—	—	800.00	760.00

Comments

Found with both the medium and heavy motto types, and Breen reports an obvious repunched mintmark variety.

The 1934-D claims the lowest overall mint state population (PCGS & NGC combined) of the 1930's issues. While this may be partially due to lack of value in lower mint state grades, the price of MS65's would certainly justify the submission of MS63 and higher coins to try for this grade.

This date is tough to find from Fine to AU. It is also one of the most underrated in the series in MS60-MS64. The 1936-D, for example, with 50% more coins graded in MS63 is valued at $300, yet the 1934-D is only $75-$100. Not to mention the 1934-D boasts the third lowest mintage in the entire series!

Expect to pay a premium for nice specimens, but still well worth the investment at current levels.

Medium Motto

Heavy Motto

1935

Mintage
Business strikes: 32,484,000

Varieties
101   Doubled die obverse. Presently considered very rare with fewer than 5 specimens known. (FS#25¢-010)

PCGS & NGC Combined Certified Populations

	MS60-62	MS63	MS64	MS65	MS66	MS67
MS	15	65	285	427	156	27

Value

	1949	1964	1979	1994	CDN
VG	—	—	1.75	1.75	—
F	—	—	2.00	2.00	1.00
VF	—	—	—	4.00	1.50
XF	—	2.25	3.50	6.00	2.25
MS60	1.75	8.00	15.00	—	14.00
MS63	—	—	—	30.00	18.00
MS65	—	—	—	75.00	60.00

1935-P Continued

Comments

Found only with medium motto obverse (see photo with accompanying 1935-D – also, Chapter 1, *Major Design Changes*).

Due to its high mintage, a large number of uncertified mint state specimens exist. It's low value, even in high grade, make this an affordable coin in MS65. At today's levels this date seems hardly worth certifying below MS65. Most of the PCGS and NGC certified coins were most likely submitted a few years ago when values were higher. The 1991 *Redbook,* for example, lists the MS65 price at $200. With the exception of a few scarce dates, this is true of almost all the Washington quarters.

1935-D

Mintage
Business strikes: 5,780,000

Varieties
Two repunched mintmark varieties are reported in *The RPM Book*.

PCGS & NGC Combined Certified Populations

	MS60-62	MS63	MS64	MS65	MS66	MS67
MS	23	73	238	139	26	2

Value

	1949	1964	1979	1994	CDN
VG	—	—	1.75	3.00	2.00
F	—	1.65	2.50	4.00	2.75
VF	—	—	—	8.00	5.00
XF	—	6.00	9.00	12.00	9.00
MS60	2.00	30.00	120.00	—	70.00
MS63	—	—	—	100.00	85.00
MS65	—	—	—	335.00	190.00

Comments

Found only with the medium motto obverse (see photo below – also, Chapter 1, *Major Design Changes*).

"The best coin in the set, hands down!", says Elliot Goldman. The 1935-D is the most underrated date in the entire Washington quarter set in mint state grades. The total mint state certified population is even lower than the 1932-D or 1932-S.* Goldman sells these coins for double their published values, when he can locate them.

The shrewd investor/collector would be wise to grab up all that can be found, but expect to pay a premium. (Some people are undoubtedly doing this already!)

Like most early mintmark dates in the series, this coin is difficult to find in grades VF to AU.

---

* The reason for this is that the 1932-D is worth certifying in all mint state grades while, at current values, the 1935-D is not — except in MS64 and above.

1935-S

Mintage
Business strikes: 5,660,000

PCGS & NGC Combined Certified Populations

	MS60-62	MS63	MS64	MS65	MS66	MS67
MS	30	131	316	233	62	9

Value

	1949	1964	1979	1994	CDN
VG	—	—	1.75	2.25	1.25
F	—	1.65	2.50	3.00	1.25
VF	—	—	—	6.00	3.50
XF	—	6.25	9.00	9.00	7.00
MS60	3.25	31.00	70.00	—	38.00
MS63	—	—	—	70.00	50.00
MS65	—	—	—	300.00	115.00

Comments
Found only with the medium motto obverse (see photo accompanying 1935-D – also, Chapter 1, *Major Design Changes*).

Readily available in low grades (AG-VG) but tough to find and undervalued in grades VF to AU. Has a similar mintage to the 1935-D but is more available in mint state. Currently undervalued in mint state, especially in MS63.

1936

Mintage
Business strikes: 41,300,000
Proof strikes: 3,837

Varieties
101   Doubled die obverse. Most noticeable at the motto.
(Breen-4281, FS # 25¢-011) *(photo)*

PCGS & NGC Combined Certified Populations

	MS60-62	MS63	MS64	MS65	MS66	MS67
MS	14	55	321	551	117	7
Proof	53	120	311	169	48	3

Value

	1949	1964	1979	1994	CDN
VF	—	—	—	2.25	1.50
XF	—	1.45	3.00	4.00	2.00
MS60	1.75	7.00	—	—	12.00
MS63	—	—	—	22.00	17.00
MS65	—	—	15.00	65.00	50.00
PR65	12.00	100.00	485.00	925.00	750.00

1936-P Continued

Comments

Found only with heavy motto obverse (see photo below – also, Chapter 1, *Major Design Changes*).

1936 was the first year since 1915 that the Mint resumed production of proof coinage. While mint state coins are readily available in all grades, the proofs are truly scarce. With less than 4 thousand minted coins, the 1936 proof is highly sought by both those completing 1936 "proof sets" and those who collect Washington quarter proofs by date. It is also prized as the first proof issue. Add to this demand the fact that 1936 proofs are mostly found with some toning or an unattractive smoky haze. (This may be a result of the mint being out of practice in the delicate handling required for such specimen coinage.) Collectors seeking a brilliant, untoned proof 1936 quarter have their work cut out for them.

101. 1936 Doubled die obverse.
(Photos courtesy of J.T. Stanton – CPG)

1936-D

Mintage
Business strikes: 5,374,000

Varieties
101   Repunched D. Several RPM's known (Breen-4284)
102   D/horizontal D. (Breen-4285)

PCGS & NGC Combined Certified Populations

	MS60-62	MS63	MS64	MS65	MS66	MS67
MS	47	149	288	145	26	2

Value

	1949	1964	1979	1994	CDN
VG	—	3.75	2.00	—	2.00
F	—	7.00	4.00	—	2.25
VF	—	—	—	14.00	11.00
XF	—	40.00	30.00	35.00	26.00
MS60	9.00	160.00	—	—	235.00
MS63	—	—	—	300.00	285.00
MS65	—	—	300.00	950.00	525.00

1936-D Continued

Comments

The third most expensive regular-issue coin in the series in all grades — except for the 1934-D which is priced higher in the *Greysheet* in MS65.

The value of gem (grades MS64 and higher) 1936-D's has suffered recently as the population of certified coins increased. The July 1991 *PCGS Population Report* shows a total mint state population of 342 coins. In May 1992 this number increased by 28 to 370. By October 1993 the population had jumped to 447. It seems that high prices brought some additional coins into the market.

Authentication of mint state specimens is recommended. A number of added-mintmark counterfeits have been seen.

Though mintage was 40% higher than that of the 1936-S, the population of mint state coins is only about half of the San Francisco issue. This is another example of the much lower survivorship in mint state of the early Denver issues compared with those from the San Francisco Mint.

The 1936-D is still a key to the set. Expect to have to search for a nice, high-end specimen, but not to pay any significant premium.

1936-S

Mintage
Business strikes: 3,828,000

PCGS & NGC Combined Certified Populations

	MS60-62	MS63	MS64	MS65	MS66	MS67
MS	20	102	478	499	92	3

Value

	1949	1964	1979	1994	CDN
VG	—	—	1.75	—	1.25
F	—	—	2.50	—	1.65
VF	—	—	—	6.00	4.00
XF	—	4.25	9.00	10.00	7.50
MS60	2.50	26.00	—	—	35.00
MS63	—	—	—	60.00	40.00
MS65	—	—	65.00	140.00	70.00

Comments
Another great bargain in the Washington quarter set, the 1936-S boasts the ninth lowest mintage but a price of less than $65 for most mint state specimens. Relative to the 1936-D, this date was saved by collectors early on. However, it still seems too cheap at current levels. The 1989 *Redbook* listed this date at $450. in MS65. Circulated coins from Fine to AU are harder to find than mint state coins and are undervalued.

1937

Mintage
Business strikes: 19,696,000
Proof strikes: 5,542

Varieties
101 Doubled die obverse. Doubling shows clearly at date and motto. (Breen-4287, FS # 25¢-012) *(photo)*

PCGS & NGC Combined Certified Populations

	MS60-62	MS63	MS64	MS65	MS66	MS67
MS	11	34	190	262	78	11
Proof	33	75	267	341	136	32

Value

	1949	1964	1979	1994	CDN
VF	—	—	—	2.25	1.50
XF	—	1.50	3.00	5.00	2.00
MS60	1.50	7.00	—	—	14.00
MS63	—	—	—	30.00	20.00
MS65	—	—	22.00	90.00	60.00
PR65	5.50	45.00	100.00	240.00	310.00

Comments

Breen reports that reverse hub B was used for the first time to strike the proof issues (see *Major Design Changes* for diagnostics). All business strikes, however, were still minted using the reverse hub A.

The *Cherrypicker's Guide* reports #101 as very rare (only 3 known) with a value of $300 in XF and $2,500 in MS60.

The 1937 boasts the lowest mintage in Philadelphia since 1932. This coin is inexpensive in mint state and, as a result, not many have been certified. The current PCGS/NGC population of mint state coins is lower than either the 1937-D or -S, both of which have much lower mintages and are much scarcer.

Proof quarters had the lowest mintage of the 1937 proof set and are in strong demand.

101. 1937 Doubled die obverse.
(Photos courtesy of J.T. Stanton – CPG)

1937-D

Mintage
Business strikes: 7,189,600

PCGS & NGC Combined Certified Populations

	MS60-62	MS63	MS64	MS65	MS66	MS67
MS	14	58	322	325	62	3

Value

	1949	1964	1979	1994	CDN
VF	—	—	—	6.00	4.00
XF	—	1.50	5.00	8.00	6.00
MS60	1.50	10.00	—	—	22.00
MS63	—	—	—	40.00	30.00
MS65	—	—	30.00	115.00	50.00

Comments
A tough coin to locate in circulated grades VF-AU, but uncirculated coins were saved in roll quantity and are available at a reasonable price. Despite the substantial population of mint state coins, these seem undervalued at present. The 1937-D carries a much lower price than the 1937-S yet has a substantially lower certified population.

1937-S

Mintage
Business strikes: 1,652,000

PCGS & NGC Combined Certified Populations

	MS60-62	MS63	MS64	MS65	MS66	MS67
MS	12	128	446	362	74	8

Value

	1949	1964	1979	1994	CDN
VF	—	—	—	11.00	8.00
XF	—	6.00	20.00	16.00	14.00
MS60	3.50	50.00	—	—	68.00
MS63	—	—	—	95.00	75.00
MS65	—	—	90.00	165.00	125.00

Comments
The third lowest mintage in the set, but with a total mint state population of over 1000 coins. Though its mintage is less than 1/4 that of the 1937-D, about 250 more coins have been certified. The only dates with a lower mintage are the 1932-D and 1932-S keys. It may not be undervalued but this date is certainly reasonable at present. Consider that the 1989 *Redbook* listed MS65 specimens at $750! Pick a nice specimen for your collection and maybe a couple of extras for the future before the price rises again.

John Feigenbaum

1938

Mintage
Business strikes: 9,472,000
Proof strikes: 8,045

PCGS & NGC Combined Certified Populations

	MS60-62	MS63	MS64	MS65	MS66	MS67
MS	11	53	221	278	77	8
Proof	35	107	365	449	204	46

Value

	1949	1964	1979	1994	CDN
VF	—	—	—	10.00	5.50
XF	—	5.00	10.00	14.00	9.00
MS60	1.50	45.00	—	—	33.00
MS63	—	—	—	50.00	40.00
MS65	—	—	50.00	120.00	65.00
PR65	3.50	45.00	95.00	150.00	250.00

Comments

Washington's profile has been sharpened slightly, most noticeably on the nose.

Only 12 million quarters were minted in 1938 (both Philadelphia and San Francisco) which is second only to 1932 as the lowest in the entire series. Compare this to recent yearly mintages measured in the billions to put this into perspective.

Goldman characterizes the 1938-P as a tough date to locate which sells for "way over current levels" — and very quickly when it is available.

Like most early Washington quarters this date is undervalued. Listed in the 1989 *Redbook* at $400 in MS65 and $550 in Proof 65. Nice white proofs are in strong demand.

1938-S

Mintage
Business strikes: 2,832,000

Varieties
101   Several RPM's reported.

PCGS & NGC Combined Certified Populations

	MS60-62	MS63	MS64	MS65	MS66	MS67
MS	10	64	322	403	86	8

Value

	1949	1964	1979	1994	CDN
VF	—	—	—	8.00	6.00
XF	—	2.75	12.00	12.00	8.50
MS60	2.25	19.00	—	—	35.00
MS63	—	—	—	50.00	40.00
MS65	—	—	45.00	120.00	75.00

Comments
Exhibits the same sharpened profile as its Philadelphia counterpart.

The 1938-S has a high survivorship in mint state, compared with the 1938-P. With a mintage of less than 1/3 that of its Philadelphia cousin there are 245 more certified coins. Still an excellent value, especially in mint state, considering it has the sixth lowest mintage in the series.

1939

Mintage

Business strikes: 33,540,000
Proof strikes: 8,795

PCGS & NGC Combined Certified Populations

	MS60-62	MS63	MS64	MS65	MS66	MS67
MS	3	24	186	379	232	47
Proof	25	72	282	478	236	62

Value

	1949	1964	1979	1994	CDN
VF	—	—	—	2.25	1.50
XF	—	1.50	3.00	4.00	1.75
MS60	1.50	8.50	—	—	10.00
MS63	—	—	—	20.00	14.00
MS65	—	—	10.00	75.00	27.00
PR65	3.00	30.00	50.00	145.00	230.00

Comments

Mintage levels increased sharply over the 12 million of 1938, perhaps in response to the United States breaking out of the depression. World War II was commencing overseas and U.S. exports increased.

Current levels are low and this is a good time to pick up a nice specimen for your collection. However, large quantities of mint state coins certainly exist and it is not recommended for investment. Nice XF and AU specimens are plentiful and can be bought for just a few dollars.

John Feigenbaum

1939-D

Mintage
Business strikes: 7,092,000

Varieties
101 Possible D/S. Very rare. (Breen-4298, FS#25¢-012.3) *(photo)*
102 RPM. Reported by Breen.

PCGS & NGC Combined Certified Populations

	MS60-62	MS63	MS64	MS65	MS66	MS67
MS	3	30	262	424	108	16

Value

	1949	1964	1979	1994	CDN
VF	—	—	—	6.00	3.00
XF	—	1.50	3.00	8.00	6.00
MS60	1.50	8.50	—	—	21.00
MS63	—	—	—	30.00	24.00
MS65	—	—	23.00	85.00	50.00

Comments

The highest mintage from Denver since the series' inception. After a one-year hiatus in 1938 the Denver Mint would produce quarters without interruption until 1965.

Probably the most common of the pre-1940 mintmarked Washington quarters in circulated as well as mint state grades. The only mintmarked date readily available in XF or AU.

101. Possible 1939-D/S.
(Photo courtesy of J.T. Stanton – CPG)

1939-S

Mintage
Business strikes: 2,628,000

Varieties
101 Doubled die obverse. Minor doubling shows east at date and motto. *(photo)*

PCGS & NGC Combined Certified Populations

	MS60-62	MS63	MS64	MS65	MS66	MS67
MS	11	54	208	274	75	10

Value

	1949	1964	1979	1994	CDN
VF	—	—	—	7.00	4.00
XF	—	3.50	10.00	10.00	8.00
MS60	2.25	24.00	—	—	40.00
MS63	—	—	—	60.00	44.00
MS65	—	—	50.00	130.00	70.00

Comments

The 1939-S is the fourth lowest mintage in the series, yet can still be bought for under $60 in mint state. Another bargain typical of this series. Current total PCGS/NGC population is only 632 coins — lower than the 1936-D! But this is partially because the coin isn't worth the submission fee of the certification services at current levels. If prices ever approach the 1991 *Redbook* level of $325 (for an MS65) more coins will likely be submitted.

Like the 1938-P, Goldman characterizes the 1939-S as a tough date to locate which sells for "way over current levels" and very quickly when available.

101. 1939-S Doubled die obverse.
(Photos courtesy of Bill Fivaz)

1940

Mintage
Business strikes: 35,704,000
Proof strikes: 11,246

PCGS & NGC Combined Certified Populations

	MS60-62	MS63	MS64	MS65	MS66	MS67
MS	1	6	62	181	183	54
Proof	27	71	328	582	290	67

Value

	1949	1964	1979	1994	CDN
VF	—	—	—	2.00	1.25
XF	—	2.25	3.00	4.00	1.50
MS60	1.25	11.00	—	—	7.00
MS63	—	—	—	17.00	13.00
MS65	—	—	10.00	37.00	30.00
PR65	2.50	20.00	32.50	130.00	175.00

Comments
As a result of America's external involvement as supplier to the Allied nations, our economy strengthened and the Mint maintained 1939 production levels. The war years would see a great increase in quarter production, exceeding 100 million coins at the Philadelphia Mint alone in 1942. From this date forward many coins exist in roll, if not bag, quantities. The coins of the 1940's remain extremely inexpensive considering their age and condition.

1940-D

Mintage
Business strikes: 2,797,600

Varieties
101 Doubled die obverse. Doubling shows clearly at motto.
(FS #25¢-012.5) *(photo)*
102 D/D/D. Totally separated to the west (FS #25¢-012.4) *(photo)*

PCGS & NGC Combined Certified Populations

	MS60-62	MS63	MS64	MS65	MS66	MS67
MS	10	60	272	339	90	3

Value

	1949	1964	1979	1994	CDN
VF	—	—	—	5.00	4.00
XF	—	4.00	12.00	11.00	8.00
MS60	2.00	27.50	—	—	44.00
MS63	—	—	—	55.00	47.00
MS65	—	—	50.00	85.00	72.00

Comments

The last mintage in the series below 3 million, the 1940-D is a very popular date among collectors. Tough to find in VF-AU but now available and quite reasonable in mint state. Uncirculated prices are bound to rise for this date. The 1989 *Redbook* listed the MS65 price of this date at $400!

Note there is almost no spread in price between MS60 and MS63. Nice MS63-64 pieces should be picked up when available.

The 1940-D, 1942-S and 1943-S together form the "big three" of the 1940-present Washington quarter set.

101. 1940-D Doubled die obverse.
(Photo courtesy of J.T. Stanton – CPG)

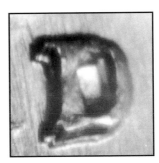

102. 1940-D/D/D west.
(Photo courtesy of J.T. Stanton – CPG, coin courtesy Lee Heimke)

1940-S

Mintage
Business strikes: 8,244,000

Varieties
101 Doubled die obverse. Doubling shows clearly at motto. (FS #25¢-012.7) *(photo)*

PCGS & NGC Combined Certified Populations

	MS60-62	MS63	MS64	MS65	MS66	MS67
MS	2	12	118	278	159	55

Value

	1949	1964	1979	1994	CDN
VF	—	—	—	2.00	1.30
XF	—	—	3.00	4.00	1.75
MS60	1.00	6.00	—	—	11.00
MS63	—	—	—	20.00	15.00
MS65	—	—	25.00	45.00	25.00

John Feigenbaum

Comments

Comes with a small S mintmark (the same used from 1932-1939). Breen reports the possibility of large S which was used from 1941 on, but its existence is not verified. Undervalued in mint state, considering its age and mintage. The 1991 *Redbook* listed MS65's at $100.

101. 1940-S Doubled die obverse.
(Photo courtesy of J.T. Stanton – CPG)

1941

Mintage
Business strikes: 79,032,000
Proof strikes: 15,287

Varieties
101   Doubled die obverse. Doubling shows south (Breen-4304, FS #25¢-012.7) *(photo)*

102   Doubled die obverse. Doubling shows northwest. (Breen-4304, FS #25¢-012.9) *(photo)*

103   Doubled die reverse. Doubling shows clearly on eagle's beak (FS #25¢-013) *(photo)*

PCGS & NGC Combined Certified Populations

	MS60-62	MS63	MS64	MS65	MS66	MS67
MS	0	3	83	110	78	68
Proof	52	85	397	731	325	57

Value

	1949	1964	1979	1994	CDN
XF	—	—	2.00	3.00	—
MS60	1.00	3.00	—	—	4.00
MS63	—	—	—	8.00	5.50
MS65	—	—	5.00	25.00	18.00
PR65	2.25	17.50	27.50	125.00	120.00

1941 Continued

Comments

With much of the world embroiled in World War II, the United States found itself in the position of supplying many goods and services to the warring nations. The economic boost put the Great Depression behind us once and for all and the demand for coinage grew as well. 1941 saw the highest-ever (to that date) mintage of quarters in our history though this number was soon exceeded. Available in all circulated grades, most for just a little over bullion value. For this and subsequent years, many below AU were melted for bullion value during the great "Hunt Brothers" silver price rise in 1979-80.

101. 1941 Doubled die obverse south.
(Photo courtesy of J.T. Stanton – CPG)

102. 1941 Doubled die obverse n.w.
(Photo courtesy of J.T. Stanton – CPG)

103. 1941 Doubled die reverse.
Beak clearly doubled.
(Photo courtesy of J.T. Stanton – CPG)

1941-D

Mintage
Business strikes: 16,714,800

Varieties
101   Doubled die obverse. Doubling shows south. Discovered by Tom Miller. (Breen-4309) *(photo)*

PCGS & NGC Combined Certified Populations

	MS60-62	MS63	MS64	MS65	MS66	MS67
MS	5	5	41	66	30	19

Value

	1949	1964	1979	1994	CDN
XF	—	—	2.50	4.00	—
MS60	1.00	4.00	—	—	11.00
MS63	—	—	—	17.00	13.00
MS65	—	—	17.50	41.00	27.00

Comments

The 1941-D marked the highest-ever (to that date) mintage at Denver and, for the collector, the first year of readily available coins in any grade through gem BU. Because of its low value, the vast majority of mint state specimens have not been submitted for certification. Therefore, finding a nice certified specimen may be tricky, though "raw" coins are plentiful. Nice mint state coins are undervalued.

101. 1941-D Doubled die obverse.
(Photo courtesy of Bill Fivaz)

1941-S

Mintage
Business strikes: 16,080,000

Varieties
101   Small S: same mintmark used from 1932-1940. (Breen-4306)
102   Large S: same mintmark used from 1942-1944. Midsection is thicker and serifs sharper than small S. (Breen-4307)

PCGS & NGC Combined Certified Populations

	MS60-62	MS63	MS64	MS65	MS66	MS67
MS	3	16	81	165	85	25

Value

	1949	1964	1979	1994	CDN
XF	—	—	2.25	3.00	—
MS60	1.25	5.00	—	—	12.00
MS63	—	—	—	20.00	15.00
MS65	—	—	14.00	41.00	55.00

Comments
Lowest of the 1941 mintages and worth nearly double its Philadelphia and Denver counterparts in MS65. In 1991 this date was listed at $85 in the Redbook and thus is a good deal at today's more reasonable levels.

1942

Mintage
Business strikes: 102,096,000
Proof strikes: 21,123

Varieties
101 Doubled die reverse. Doubling shows clearly on reverse lettering (FS #25¢-014) *(photo)*
102 Doubled die reverse. Doubling shows clearly on reverse lettering. Possibly unique. (FS #25¢-014.3) *(photo)*

PCGS & NGC Combined Certified Populations

	MS60-62	MS63	MS64	MS65	MS66	MS67
MS	0	10	45	58	62	24
Proof	56	135	611	1021	402	54

Value

	1949	1964	1979	1994	CDN
XF	—	—	1.50	3.00	—
MS60	.75	3.00	—	—	4.00
MS63	—	—	—	8.00	5.50
MS65	—	—	4.00	30.00	16.00
PR65	2.00	16.00	27.50	125.00	120.00

1942 Continued

Comments

Again the Mint set a new record for mintage in response to increased economic activity as the United States entered World War II. Don't let the low PCGS/NGC populations fool you — this date is readily available in mint state. It's just not worth having certified.

101. 1942 Doubled die reverse.
(Photo courtesy of J.T. Stanton – CPG)

102. 1942 Doubled die reverse. Only known specimen.
(Photos courtesy of J.T. Stanton – CPG; coin courtesy Geoff Fults)

1942-D

Mintage
Business strikes: 17,487,200

Varieties
101   Doubled die obverse. Doubling shows clearly to the north on the motto and to the west on LIBERTY. (Breen-4315, FS #25¢-015) *(photo)*

102   Doubled die reverse. Dramatic doubling shows plainly on arrows and olive branch; eagle's beak is also clearly doubled. (Breen-4316, FS #25¢-016) *(photo)*

PCGS & NGC Combined Certified Populations

	MS60-62	MS63	MS64	MS65	MS66	MS67
MS	6	36	52	50	26	5

Value

	1949	1964	1979	1994	CDN
XF	—	—	2.50	4.00	—
MS60	1.00	2.50	—	—	7.75
MS63	—	—	—	12.00	9.00
MS65	—	—	17.50	35.00	22.00

1942-D Continued

Comments

With the low population of PCGS/NGC coins, collectors will have a difficult time finding a nice certified coin for a "slab" set. However, raw mint state coins are available and highly underrated at current levels.

Bill Fivaz considers the doubled die obverse (101) one of the most sought-after Washington quarter varieties.

101. 1942-D Doubled die obverse.
(Photos courtesy of J.T. Stanton – CPG)

102. 1942-D Doubled die reverse.
(Photos courtesy of J.T. Stanton – CPG)

John Feigenbaum

1942-S

Mintage
Business strikes: 19,384,000

Varieties
101   Large S with sharp serifs. (Breen-4312)
102   Large, knob-tailed S. (Breen-4313)

PCGS & NGC Combined Certified Populations

	MS60-62	MS63	MS64	MS65	MS66	MS67
MS	9	52	180	202	74	12

Value

	1949	1964	1979	1994	CDN
XF	—	—	2.25	7.00	—
MS60	1.25	8.00	—	—	40.00
MS63	—	—	—	65.00	50.00
MS65	—	—	14.00	110.00	80.00

Comments

Breen notes the possibility of a small S mintmark (see 1941-S #101).

In 1991 this date listed at $250 in MS65 *(Redbook)*. With a mintage of 3 million more coins and a PCGS/NGC population considerably higher than the 1941-S, this date is one of the few in the set which is fully priced at present.

The 1942-S, 1940-D and 1943-S together form the "big three" of the 1940-present Washington quarter set.

1943

Mintage
Business strikes: 99,700,000

Varieties
101   Doubled die obverse. Doubling shows west. (FS#25¢-016.5)
(photo)

PCGS & NGC Combined Certified Populations

	MS60-62	MS63	MS64	MS65	MS66	MS67
MS	1	13	40	129	130	62

Value

	1949	1964	1979	1994	CDN
XF	—	—	1.50	3.00	—
MS60	.75	1.35	—	—	3.00
MS63	—	—	—	6.00	5.00
MS65	—	—	3.75	25.00	18.00

Comments

Mintage remains high as a result of America's continued involvement in the war effort. Because of this increased burden, the Mint discontinued proof coinage and would not resume again until 1950.

101. 1943 Doubled die obverse.
(Photo courtesy of J.T. Stanton –
CPG, coin courtesy Richard Pawley)

1943-D

Mintage
Business strikes: 16,095,600

Varieties

101 D/horizontal D: mintmark was first erroneously turned 90° CCW with the flat side on bottom. Second D then correctly placed over. (Breen-4321)

102 Multiple D's: as many as 4 or 5 mintmarks can be detected. (Breen-4322)

PCGS & NGC Combined Certified Populations

	MS60-62	MS63	MS64	MS65	MS66	MS67
MS	1	4	48	74	57	25

Value

	1949	1964	1979	1994	CDN
XF	—	—	2.50	4.00	—
MS60	.75	2.00	—	—	9.00
MS63	—	—	—	10.00	12.00
MS65	—	—	9.00	30.00	23.00

Comments
A good date that hasn't been slabbed much because of low values. Buy all the mint state coins you can in the $10-$15 range. They won't get cheaper.

1943-S

Mintage
Business strikes: 21,700,000

Varieties
101 Doubled die obverse. Bold doubling shows south on motto. Also shows at date and LIBERTY. (Breen-4319, FS#25¢-017) *(photo)*

PCGS & NGC Combined Certified Populations

	MS60-62	MS63	MS64	MS65	MS66	MS67
Normal	1	6	116	273	118	32
DDO	2	8	16	2	1	0

Value

	1949	1964	1979	1994	CDN
XF	—	—	2.50	4.00	—
MS60	.85	4.00	—	—	20.00
MS63	—	—	—	30.00	22.00
MS65	—	—	14.00	75.00	24.00

Comments

Double die obverse recognized by all major grading services. Typical mintmark is the large S with sharp serifs. Knob-tailed, large S may also exist.[9]

The substantial PCGS/NGC population shows that this coin was once worth considerably more — $135 in 1991 *(Redbook)*. A bargain today, especially near CDN levels. Look for flashy white specimens and put them away.

101. 1943-S Doubled die obverse.
(Photos courtesy of J.T. Stanton – CPG)

1944

Mintage
Business strikes: 104,956,000

PCGS & NGC Combined Certified Populations

	MS60-62	MS63	MS64	MS65	MS66	MS67
MS	1	4	34	101	59	44

Value

	1949	1964	1979	1994	CDN
XF	—	—	1.50	1.75	—
MS60	.60	1.50	—	—	2.25
MS63	—	—	—	6.00	4.00
MS65	—	—	4.00	15.00	10.00

Comments
Breen notes a new hub for all the 1944 coinage. Diagnostics include the sharpened queue, larger designer's initials and a slightly modified profile.

Once again the mint has increased mintage in reaction to the war effort, setting a new record for quarters. Mintage figures for the quarters would not get this high again until 1962.

Available in all grades G-MS65, though many were melted in 1979-80.

1944-D

Mintage
Business strikes: 14,600,800

PCGS & NGC Combined Certified Populations

	MS60-62	MS63	MS64	MS65	MS66	MS67
MS	0	1	31	79	60	50

Value

	1949	1964	1979	1994	CDN
XF	—	—	1.50	2.00	—
MS60	.60	1.50	—	—	6.00
MS63	—	—	—	10.00	7.50
MS65	—	—	5.00	25.00	17.00

Comments
Breen notes a new hub for all the 1944 coinage. Diagnostics include the sharpened queue, larger designer's initials and a slightly modified profile.

This begins a series of mintmarked dates in the 1940's which can be obtained in mint state for the price of lunch at a fast-food restaurant. Put a few away – they can't get cheaper!
The certified coins were all submitted when prices were higher in 1989-1991.

1944-S

Mintage
Business strikes: 12,560,000

Varieties
101 Doubled die obverse. Light doubling shows south.
(Breen-4309, FS#25¢-017.5) *(photo)*

PCGS & NGC Combined Certified Populations

	MS60-62	MS63	MS64	MS65	MS66	MS67
MS	0	6	60	130	117	79

Value

	1949	1964	1979	1994	CDN
XF	—	—	2.50	2.00	—
MS60	.65	2.60	—	—	6.00
MS63	—	—	—	11.00	8.00
MS65	—	—	8.00	27.00	20.00

Comments
See Comments for 1944-D.

101. 1944-S Doubled die obverse.
(Photo courtesy of J.T. Stanton – CPG)

1945

Mintage
Business strikes: 74,372,000

Varieties
101 Doubled die obverse. Slight doubling northwest visible on motto. (Breen-4328) *(photo)*

PCGS & NGC Combined Certified Populations

	MS60-62	MS63	MS64	MS65	MS66	MS67
MS	0	4	17	30	31	32

Value

	1949	1964	1979	1994	CDN
XF	—	—	1.50	1.75	—
MS60	.50	1.35	—	—	2.00
MS63	—	—	—	4.00	3.75
MS65	—	—	2.50	16.00	11.00

Comments

Designer's initials have been sharpened.[10]

Mintage has been lowered for the first time since 1940 — as war activities came to a close.

101. 1945 Doubled die obverse.
(Photo courtesy of J.T. Stanton – CPG)

1945-D

Mintage
Business strikes: 12,341,600

PCGS & NGC Combined Certified Populations

	MS60-62	MS63	MS64	MS65	MS66	MS67
MS	0	2	25	53	53	43

Value

	1949	1964	1979	1994	CDN
XF	—	—	1.50	1.75	—
MS60	.50	1.35	—	—	5.75
MS63	—	—	—	9.00	6.25
MS65	—	—	5.50	27.00	17.00

Comments
See Comments for 1944-D.

1945-S

Mintage
Business strikes: 17,004,001

Varieties
101   S/S northwest. (Breen-4329) *(photo)*

PCGS & NGC Combined Certified Populations

	MS60-62	MS63	MS64	MS65	MS66	MS67
MS	0	6	18	96	106	36

Value

	1949	1964	1979	1994	CDN
XF	—	—	1.50	1.75	—
MS60	.50	1.75	—	—	4.00
MS63	—	—	—	6.00	5.50
MS65	—	—	3.50	22.00	14.00

Comments
Comes with trumpet-tailed S. Breen notes that a few minutely doubled-die obverse coins may exist.

See Comments for 1944-D.

101. 1945-S/S.
(Photo courtesy of Bill Fivaz, coin courtesy of Don Lommler)

1946

Mintage
Business strikes: 53,436,000

Varieties
101   Doubled die obverse. Slight doubling apparent at date and
       motto. *(photo)*
102   Doubled die reverse. Most visible in STATES and E
       PLURIBUS UNUM. (FS#25¢-018.2) *(photo)*

PCGS & NGC Combined Certified Populations

	MS60-62	MS63	MS64	MS65	MS66	MS67
MS	0	2	10	31	32	19

Value

	1949	1964	1979	1994	CDN
XF	—	—	1.50	1.75	—
MS60	.40	1.35	—	—	3.50
MS63	—	—	—	5.00	4.00
MS65	—	—	3.25	12.00	11.00

Comments

Mintage at Philadelphia has continued to decline from the 1944 high.

101. 1946 Doubled die obverse.
(Photos courtesy Bill Fivaz)

102. 1946 Doubled die reverse.
(Photo courtesy of J.T. Stanton –
CPG, coin courtesy of Geoff Fults)

1946-D

Mintage
Business strikes: 9,072,800

Varieties
101 DDR. Doubling most noticeable in STATES OF. (Breen-4337)
102 D/S. (Breen-4336)

PCGS & NGC Combined Certified Populations

	MS60-62	MS63	MS64	MS65	MS66	MS67
MS	0	5	16	67	43	58

Value

	1949	1964	1979	1994	CDN
XF	—	—	1.50	1.75	—
MS60	.40	1.10	—	—	2.50
MS63	—	—	—	6.00	3.50
MS65	—	—	7.00	11.00	9.00

Comments
See Comments for 1944-D.

1946-S

Mintage
Business strikes: 4,204,000

Varieties
101 Trumpet-tailed S. (Breen-4333)
102 Knob-tailed S. (Breen-4334)

PCGS & NGC Combined Certified Populations

	MS60-62	MS63	MS64	MS65	MS66	MS67
MS	0	2	10	76	77	64

Value

	1949	1964	1979	1994	CDN
XF	—	—	2.00	1.75	—
MS60	.40	2.75	—	—	2.00
MS63	—	—	—	6.00	4.00
MS65	—	—	5.50	22.00	14.00

Comments
According to Breen, the knob-tailed mintmark is tougher to locate than its trumpet-tailed counterpart.

The second lowest mintage of regular-issue quarters from this date to present. Mint state coins seem ridiculously cheap at today's levels.

1947

Mintage
Business strikes: 22,556,000

PCGS & NGC Combined Certified Populations

	MS60-62	MS63	MS64	MS65	MS66	MS67
MS	0	0	11	75	70	43

Value

	1949	1964	1979	1994	CDN
XF	—	—	1.50	1.75	—
MS60	.35	1.10	—	—	4.25
MS63	—	—	—	6.00	5.25
MS65	—	—	2.75	10.00	10.00

Comments
1947 marks the first year the government issued so-call "Mint Sets" which contained one each of the cent, nickel, dime, quarter and half dollar from the Philadelphia and Denver Mints. Collectors of beautifully-toned coins pay large premiums for examples which resulted from sitting in government holders for a long period of time. Proof set production would not resume until 1950.

1947-D

Mintage
Business strikes: 15,338,400

PCGS & NGC Combined Certified Populations

	MS60-62	MS63	MS64	MS65	MS66	MS67
MS	0	2	17	91	96	139

Value

	1949	1964	1979	1994	CDN
XF	—	—	1.50	1.75	—
MS60	.35	1.35	—	—	3.25
MS63	—	—	—	5.00	5.75
MS65	—	—	3.00	12.00	11.00

Comments
Mint sets insured the survivorship of a substantial number of brilliant uncirculated coins.

1947-S

Mintage
Business strikes: 5,532,000

Varieties
101   Trumpet-tailed S. (Breen-4339)
102   Knob-tailed S. (Breen-4340)

PCGS & NGC Combined Certified Populations

	MS60-62	MS63	MS64	MS65	MS66	MS67
MS	0	4	47	161	152	191

Value

	1949	1964	1979	1994	CDN
XF	—	—	2.00	1.75	—
MS60	.35	2.00	—	—	3.00
MS63	—	—	—	5.00	4.00
MS65	—	—	4.00	10.00	13.00

Comments
According to Breen, the knob-tailed mintmark is tougher to locate than its trumpet-tailed counterpart.

Second lowest mintage since 1940-D. Generally underrated, especially since they were not included in the mint sets.

1948

Mintage
Business strikes: 35,196,000

PCGS & NGC Combined Certified Populations

	MS60-62	MS63	MS64	MS65	MS66	MS67
MS	1	1	22	70	83	58

Value

	1949	1964	1979	1994	CDN
XF	—	—	1.50	1.75	—
MS60	.35	1.25	—	—	2.25
MS63	—	—	—	4.00	5.50
MS65	—	—	2.25	11.00	8.00

Comments
See Comments on 1947-P.

1948-D

Mintage
Business strikes: 16,766,800

PCGS & NGC Combined Certified Populations

	MS60-62	MS63	MS64	MS65	MS66	MS67
MS	0	3	19	37	34	24

Value

	1949	1964	1979	1994	CDN
XF	—	—	1.50	1.75	—
MS60	.35	1.25	—	—	3.00
MS63	—	—	—	6.00	4.00
MS65	—	—	3.00	10.00	10.00

Comments
See Comments on 1947-P and 1944-D.

1948-S

Mintage
Business strikes: 15,960,000

PCGS & NGC Combined Certified Populations

	MS60-62	MS63	MS64	MS65	MS66	MS67
MS	1	5	44	99	70	82

Value

	1949	1964	1979	1994	CDN
XF	—	—	1.50	1.75	—
MS60	.35	1.60	—	—	3.25
MS63	—	—	—	6.00	6.00
MS65	—	—	2.75	15.00	13.00

Comments
Knob-tailed S mintmark used from this point on. Breen also notes the possible existence of a trumpet-tailed S in the transition.

No S-mint coin made again until 1950.

Also see Comments on 1944-D.

1949

Mintage
Business strikes: 9,312,000

PCGS & NGC Combined Certified Populations

	MS60-62	MS63	MS64	MS65	MS66	MS67
MS	1	4	35	152	130	34

Value

	1949	1964	1979	1994	CDN
XF	—	—	3.00	1.75	—
MS60	.35	5.50	—	—	13.00
MS63	—	—	—	21.00	16.00
MS65	—	—	16.00	30.00	20.00

Comments
The most valuable regular issue since 1943-S. Note mintage for this year is the lowest in Philadelphia since 1932. Also see Comments on 1947-P.

1949-D

Mintage
Business strikes: 10,068,400

PCGS & NGC Combined Certified Populations

	MS60-62	MS63	MS64	MS65	MS66	MS67
MS	0	1	28	102	88	29

Value

	1949	1964	1979	1994	CDN
XF	—	—	2.25	1.75	—
MS60	.35	2.00	—	—	5.00
MS63	—	—	—	10.00	7.00
MS65	—	—	8.00	22.00	16.00

Comments
See Comments on 1947-P.

1950

Mintage
Business strikes: 24,920,126
Proof strikes: 51,386

Varieties
101 Doubled die reverse. Eagle's beak doubled. (FS#25¢-019)
(photo)

PCGS & NGC Combined Certified Populations

	MS60-62	MS63	MS64	MS65	MS66	MS67
MS	0	2	11	47	46	76
Proof	10	36	214	531	352	104

Value

	1964	1979	1994	CDN
MS60	1.50	2.50	—	—
MS63	—	—	4.00	1.90
MS65	—	—	8.00	—
PR65	14.00	25.00	70.00	47.00

1950 Continued

Comments

The Mint made proof coinage for the first time since 1942. Proofs of this year were heavily saved because collectors had been deprived of them for eight years. Proof production is low compared with modern issues and would rise slowly until 1956. In 1957 more than 1 million proofs were issued for the first time.

Also see Comments on 1947-P.

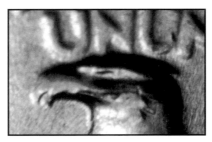

101. 1950 Doubled die reverse.
(Photo courtesy of J.T. Stanton – CPG)

1950-D

Mintage
Business strikes (all types): 21,075,600

Varieties
101 Doubled die reverse. Arrows and mintmark clearly doubled.
(Breen-4353, FS#25¢-020) *(photo)*

PCGS & NGC Combined Certified Populations

	MS60-62	MS63	MS64	MS65	MS66	MS67
MS	1	4	19	50	47	81

Value

	1964	1979	1994	CDN
XF	—	1.50	1.75	—
MS60	1.25	—	—	—
MS63	—	—	4.00	2.10
MS65	—	4.00	8.00	—

Comments
Also see 1950-D/S.

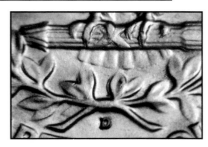

101. 1950-D Doubled die reverse.
(Photo courtesy of J.T. Stanton – CPG)

1950-D/S

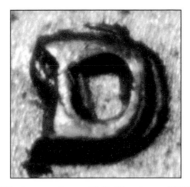

(Photo courtesy of J.T. Stanton – CPG)

Mintage
Unknown

PCGS & NGC Combined Certified Populations

	MS60-62	MS63	MS64	MS65	MS66	MS67
MS	0	9	17	7	0	0

Value

	1964	1979	1994	CDN
F	—	—	—	24.00
VF	—	—	60.00	45.00
XF	—	—	150.00	110.00
MS60	—	—	—	200.00
MS63	—	—	350.00	245.00
MS65	—	—	500.00	395.00

Comments
(Breen-4354, FS#25¢-021) Found most often in low grades where the price is very affordable. Mint state specimens are highly sought after and carry a price tag to match.

This variety was produced by the coiner placing a D mintmark over an existing S. Fivaz and Stanton suggest that this was done erroneously. The "S" shows most noticeably at the upper left where the upper curve protrudes behind the D *(photo)*.

1950-S

Mintage
Business strikes (all types): 10,284,004

PCGS & NGC Combined Certified Populations

	MS60-62	MS63	MS64	MS65	MS66	MS67
MS	1	5	17	50	61	32

Value

	1964	1979	1994	CDN
XF	—	1.50	1.75	—
MS60	2.60	—	—	—
MS63	—	—	7.00	4.75
MS65	—	6.00	16.00	—

Comments
Also see 1950-S/D.

1950-S/D

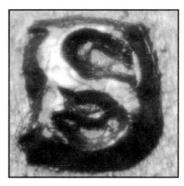

(Photo courtesy of J.T. Stanton – CPG)

Mintage
Unknown

PCGS & NGC Combined Certified Populations

	MS60-62	MS63	MS64	MS65	MS66	MS67
MS	1	1	15	19	3	2

Value

	1964	1979	1994	CDN
F	—	—	—	24.00
VF	—	—	65.00	45.00
XF	—	—	175.00	135.00
MS60	—	—	—	325.00
MS63	—	—	550.00	350.00
MS65	—	—	625.00	450.00

Comments
(Breen-4351, FS#25¢-021) As with the 1950-D/S, found most often in low grades where the price is affordable. Mint state specimens are highly sought after and carry a price tag to match.

Created in similar fashion to the D/S variety. Shows quite clearly under magnification *(photo)*.

1951

Mintages & Values

	Mintage	1994 MS65 & PR65 Redbook	CDN
1951	43,448,102	$ 7.00	$ 2.15
1951 Proof	57,500	45.00	27.00
1951-D	35,354.800	5.00	1.95
1951-S	9,048,000	23.00	13.00

Varieties

101 1951-D/D with doubled die obverse. (FS#25¢-017) *(photo)*
102 1951-D/S. (Breen-4358)

Comments

Business strikes come with reverse type A and proofs with reverse type B. (Refer to Chapter 1, *Major Design Changes* for more information on reverse hub types.)[11]

Production at the Denver mint is starting to expand.

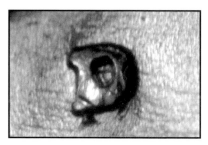

101. 1951-D/D with doubled die obverse.
(Photo courtesy of J.T. Stanton – CPG)

1952

Mintages & Values

	Mintage	1994 MS65 & PR65 Redbook	CDN
1952	38,780,183	$ 6.00	$ 1.75
1952 Proof	81,980	35.00	23.00
1952-D	49,795,200	7.50	1.70
1952-S	13,707,800	12.00	6.50

Varieties

101   1952 Proof. Doubled reverse hub B struck over hub A. (Breen-4360)

Comments

More production at the Denver mint than Philadelphia for only the second time in the series (first in 1949).

1953

Mintages & Values

	Mintage	1994 MS65 & PR65 Redbook	CDN
1953	18,536,120	$ 7.50	$ 1.50
1953 Proof	128,800	25.00	16.00
1953-D	56,112,400	4.00	.95
1953-S	9,048,000	6.00	1.65

Varieties

101 1953-D/D/D/S. (FS#25¢-022.2, Breen-4367) *(photo)*
102 1953-D. Doubled die reverse. (FS#25¢-022.2) *(photo)*

Comments

The vast majority of production is at Denver — a pattern that repeats from 1957 through 1964.

101. 1953-D/D/D/S
(Photo courtesy of Bill Fivaz)

102. 1953-D Doubled die reverse.
(Photo courtesy of J.T. Stanton – CPG)

102. 1953-D Doubled die reverse.
(Photo courtesy of J.T. Stanton – CPG)

1954

Mintages & Values

	Mintage	1994 MS65 & PR65 Redbook	CDN
1954	54,412,203	$ 4.00	$ ..95
1954 Proof	233,300	17.00	10.00
1954-D	42,305,500	4.00	.95
1954-S	11,834,722	5.00	.95

Comments

Last year of San Francisco Mint production of regular coinage. Starting in 1968, San Francisco would take over the manufacture of proof coinage.

1955

Mintages & Values

	Mintage	1994 MS65 & PR65 Redbook	CDN
1955	18,180,181	$ 4.50	$ .95
1955 Proof	378,200	12.00	9.00
1955-D	3,182,400	6.00	1.10

Comments

The mintage for both mints is the lowest since 1949 and fourth lowest in the entire series.

The 1955-D has a particularly low mintage and has probably been heavily saved because of this.

About halfway through the production year, the Mint began shipping proof sets in polyethylene plastic envelopes (called "flat" sets) instead of the previously-used boxes. The flat sets would be used until 1966 when the Mint would begin packaging the sets in hard plastic.

1956

Mintages & Values

	Mintage	1994 MS65 & PR65 Redbook	CDN
1956	44,144,000	$ 3.25	$ .95
1956 Proof	669,384	5.00	5.00
1956-D	32,334,500	3.25	1.05

Varieties

101   1956-D/horizontal D (?). (Breen-4378)

Comments

While all business strikes on the Philadelphia coins were supposed to be struck with hub A, Breen notes that a few were struck with reverse type B and are rare. Reverse B was primarily used for proof coinage. The Denver coins were struck with both hub types. Neither is scarce.

1957

Mintages & Values

	Mintage	1994 MS65 & PR65 Redbook	CDN
1957	46,532,000	$ 3.25	$ .95
1957 Proof	1,247,952	4.50	3.15
1957-D	77,924,160	3.25	.95

Comments

While all business strikes on the Philadelphia coins were supposed to be struck with hub A, Breen notes that approximately 5% were struck with reverse type B. Reverse B was primarily used for proof coinage. The Denver coins were struck with both hub types. Neither is scarce.

First time proof production is over 1 million.

1958

Mintages & Values

	Mintage	1994 MS65 & PR65 Redbook	CDN
1958	6,360,000	$ 5.50	$ .95
1958 Proof	875,652	6.00	4.75
1958-D	78,124,900	3.25	.95

Comments

A small portion of the business strike mintage of the Philadelphia coinage and all proofs were struck with the type B reverse. The Denver coins were struck with both reverse hub types. Neither is scarce.[12]

Lowest production at the Philadelphia Mint since 1932.

1959

Mintages & Values

	Mintage	1994 MS65 & PR65 Redbook	CDN
1959	24,384,000	$ 3.25	$ .95
1959 Proof	1,149,291	5.00	3.25
1959-D	62,054,232	3.25	.95

Varieties
101   1959 Proof. Doubled die obverse. *(photo)*

Comments
A small portion of the business strike mintage of the Philadelphia coinage (including all mint set coins) and all proofs were struck with the type B reverse. The Denver coins were struck with both reverse hub types. Neither is scarce.[13]

101. 1959 Proof doubled die obverse.
(Photo courtesy of Bill Fivaz)

John Feigenbaum

1960

Mintages & Values

	Mintage	1994 MS65 & PR65 Redbook	CDN
1960	29,164,000	$ 3.25	$ .95
1960 Proof	1,691,602	4.50	3.00
1960-D	63,000324	3.25	.95

Varieties

101   1960 Proof Double Die Reverse (FS#25¢-022.5) *(photo)*

Comments

A small portion of the business strike mintage of the Philadelphia coinage (including some of the mint set coins) and all proofs were struck with the type B reverse. The Denver coins were struck with both reverse hub types. Neither is scarce.[14]

101. 1960 Doubled die obverse.
(Photo courtesy of J.T. Stanton – CPG, coin courtesy Del Romines)

1961

Mintages & Values

	Mintage	1994 MS65 & PR65 Redbook	CDN
1961	37,036,000	$ 3.25	$ .95
1961 Proof	3,028,244	4.50	2.75
1961-D	83,656,928	3.25	.95

Comments
See Comments for 1960.

1962

Mintages & Values

	Mintage	1994 MS65 & PR65 Redbook	CDN
1962	36,156,000	$ 3.25	$ .95
1962 Proof	3,218,019	4.50	2.75
1962-D	127,554,756	3.25	.95

Varieties
101   1962-D/horizontal D. (Breen-4404)

Comments
See Comments for 1960.

John Feigenbaum

1963

Mintages & Values

	Mintage	1994 MS65 & PR65 Redbook	CDN
1963	74,316,000	$ 3.25	$ .95
1963 Proof	3,075,645	4.50	2.75
1963-D	135,288,184	3.25	.95

Varieties

101   1963-P. Doubled die obverse. (FS#25¢-023) *(photo)*
102   1963-P. Doubled die obverse & reverse. (FS#25¢-024) *(photo)*
103   1963-D. Doubled die obverse. (Breen-4408)

Comments

See Comments for 1960.
Rolls of mint state coins are hoarded for their silver content.

101 & 103. 1963 Doubled die obverse.
(Photo courtesy of J.T. Stanton – CPG)

102 & 103. 1934 Doubled die reverse.
(Photo courtesy of J.T. Stanton – CPG)

1964

Mintages & Values

	Mintage	1994 MS65 & PR65 Redbook	CDN
1964	560,390,585	$ 3.25	$ .95
1964 Proof	3,950,762	4.50	2.75
1964-D	704,135,528	3.25	.95

Varieties

101 1964. Doubled die reverse. (FS#25¢-024.5) *(photo)*
102 1964-D. Doubled die reverse. (FS#25¢-025) *(photo)*

Comments

See Comments for 1960. A third, type C, reverse probably exists on business strikes from both mints which Breen calls "transitional" pieces. Reverse C was used from 1965 - present. He also reports a 1964 piece struck on a clad planchet.[15] Also, the last year proofs would be minted until 1968.

This is the last year of regular-issue 90% silver coinage in the United States. Production exceeded 1 billion quarters for the first time. The proof set production of 4 million is also the highest to date and would not be exceeded until the Bicentennial issue of 1976.

Rolls, and even bags, of these silver quarters are commonly hoarded as a silver investment. Even in mint state 1964 quarters tend to carry no premium over bullion value.

101. 1964 Doubled die reverse.
(Photo courtesy CPG, Don Lommler)

102. 1964-D Doubled die reverse.
(Photo courtesy CPG, Don Lommler)

THE CLAD COINAGE
1965-PRESENT

1965

Mintages & Values

	Mintage	1994 MS65 & PR65 Redbook	CDN
1965	1,819,717,540	.85	.35
1965 sms*	2,360,000	—	.40

* sms - Special Mint Sets were produced by the San Francisco Mint (without mintmarks). Mint state coins have a proof-like surface.

Varieties

101   1965. Doubled die obverse. (FS#25¢-026) *(photo)*

Comments

1965 marked the first year of issue for Washington quarters struck on the new clad or "sandwich" metal planchets. The Mint abandoned the previous silver standard in response to the high price of silver. The melt value of pre-1965 coins soon exceeded their face value and virtually all disappeared from circulation overnight. Production in this and subsequent years was very high to replace the silver coins which were no longer being used. Clad coins can be distinguished easily by the copper-colored band along the edge. These new coins were found to be acceptable for vending machines, which was a significant consideration at the time. The decision proved unpopular with numismatists, however, because the new metal looked "shiny", did not show as much detail and was apparently far easier to counterfeit on a large scale.

The Denver mint also produced coins this year, however no mintmark was added so these are indistinguishable from the Philadelphia issues. No proofs were minted.

In addition to the new planchets, a new reverse hub C was put into use and is found on all 1965 quarters. Breen reports the existence of a 1965 coin struck on a silver planchet, which is very rare and possibly unique.

101. 1965 Doubled die obverse.
(Photos courtesy of J.T. Stanton – CPG)

1966

Mintages & Values

	Mintage	1994 MS65 & PR65 Redbook	CDN
1966	821,101,500	.85	.40
1966 sms*	2,261,583	—	.60

* sms - Special Mint Sets were produced by the San Francisco Mint (without mintmarks). Mint state coins have a proof-like surface.

Comments
All coins struck with type C reverse.[16]

1967

Mintages & Values

	Mintage	1994 MS65 & PR65 Redbook	CDN
1967	1,524,031,848	.85	.45
1967 sms*	1,863,344	—	.65

* sms - Special Mint Sets were produced by the San Francisco Mint (without mintmarks). Mint state coins have a proof-like surface.

Varieties
101   1967 sms. Doubled die obverse. (FS#25¢-026.5) *(photo)*

101. 1967 sms Doubled die obverse.
(Photos courtesy of J.T. Stanton – CPG)

1968

Mintages & Values

	Mintage	1994 MS65 & PR65 Redbook	CDN
1968	220,731,500	$ .85	$ .45
1968-D	101,534,000	.85	.60
1968-S Proof	3,041,506	1.50	.65

Varieties
101   1968 proof. Doubled die reverse. (FS#25¢-027) *(photo)*

Comments
The Mint restored mintmarks (removed after 1964) and placed them on the obverse of the coin behind Washington's ribbon queue *(photo)*. Proofs were also reinstated this year and minted entirely in the San Francisco Assay Office (the old Mint office) which mints, packs and distributes all proof coinage to this day.

101. 1968-S Doubled die reverse.
(Photo courtesy of CPG)

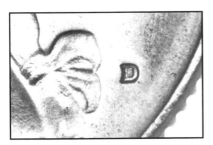

1968-D Close-up of new mintmark
location behind ribbon queue

1968-S Proof, die gouges on face.
(Photo courtesy of Bill Fivaz)

1969

Mintages & Values

	Mintage	1994 MS65 & PR65 Redbook	CDN
1969	176,212,000	$ .85	$ .50
1969-D	114,372,000	.85	.50
1969-S Proof	2,934,631	1.50	.65

Comments

Type C reverse was used on all Philadelphia business strikes and primarily on the Denver issues. Breen reports that fewer than 1% of the Denver issues were produced with the type B reverse which makes them very scarce. The type B reverse was used exclusively on the S-mint coinage.

John Feigenbaum

1970

Mintages & Values

	Mintage	1994 MS65 & PR65 Redbook	CDN
1970	136,420,000	$ .50	$ .40
1970-D	417,341,364	.50	.40
1970-S Proof	2,632,810	1.50	.60

Varieties

101   1970. Doubled die reverse.
102   1970-D. Doubled die obverse. Breen reports that many DDO varieties exist for this date.
103   1970-D. Doubled die reverse. (FS#25¢-027.3) *(photo)*

Comments

Type C reverse was used on all Philadelphia business strikes and primarily on the Denver issues. Breen reports that fewer than 0.1% of the Denver issues were produced with the type B reverse which makes them very scarce. As with the 1969 proofs, the type B reverse was used exclusively on the S-mint coinage.

101. 1970-D Doubled die obverse.
(Photos courtesy of J.T. Stanton – CPG)

1970

Mintages & Values

	Mintage	1994 MS65 & PR65 Redbook	CDN
1970	136,420,000	$ .50	$ .40
1970-D	417,341,364	.50	.40
1970-S Proof	2,632,810	1.50	.60

Varieties

101 1970. Doubled die reverse.

102 1970-D. Doubled die obverse. Breen reports that many DDO varieties exist for this date.

103 1970-D. Doubled die reverse. (FS#25¢-027.3) *(photo)*

Comments

Type C reverse was used on all Philadelphia business strikes and primarily on the Denver issues. Breen reports that fewer than 0.1% of the Denver issues were produced with the type B reverse which makes them very scarce. As with the 1969 proofs, the type B reverse was used exclusively on the S-mint coinage.

John Feigenbaum

1971

Mintages & Values

	Mintage	1994 MS65 & PR65 Redbook	CDN
1971	109,284,000	$ .50	$ .45
1971-D	258,634,428	.50	.70
1971-S Proof	3,220,733	1.50	.70

Varieties

101 1971. Doubled die reverse. (FS#25¢-027.7) *(photo)*

102 1971-D. Doubled die reverse. Several different DDR exist. (FS#25¢-027.8) *(photo)*

Comments

Type C reverse was used on all Philadelphia business strikes and primarily on the Denver issues. Breen reports that a few of the Denver issues have been reported with the type B reverse and these are rare. As with the 1969 proofs, the type B reverse was used exclusively on the S-mint coinage.

101. 1971 Doubled die reverse.
(Photo courtesy of J.T. Stanton – CPG)

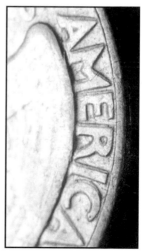

102. 1971-D Doubled die reverse.
(Photo courtesy of J.T. Stanton – CPG)

1972-1974

Mintages & Values

	Mintage	1994 MS65 & PR65 Redbook	CDN
1972	215,048,000	$ .50	$ .30
1972-D	311,067,732	.50	.45
1972-S Proof	3,260,996	1.50	.80
1973	346,924,000	$ .65	$ .45
1973-D	232,977,400	.75	.45
1973-S Proof	2,760,339	1.50	.65
1974	801,456,000	$ .70	$ .35
1974-D	353,160,300	.75	.45
1974-S Proof	2,612,568	1.50	.65

Varieties

101 1974-S/S Proof. Obvious doubled mintmark. (Breen-4445)

Comments

In 1972 the type C reverse was used on all Philadelphia business strikes and primarily on the Denver issues. Breen reports that a few of the Denver issues have been reported with the type B reverse and these are rare. The type B reverse was used exclusively on the S-mint coinage.

As of 1973 the Mint fully adopted the type C reverse and it has been used through today's coinage, with the exception of the Bicentennial reverse in 1976.

No coins were minted bearing the date 1975 in preparation for the forthcoming Bicentennial coins. To compensate for this void, 1974-dated quarters were produced through 1975 which is one reason why the total yearly mintage was one of the highest ever for quarters to that time. (Bicentennial quarters, which were also were minted in 1975, had a total mintage of 1.6+ billion which was the second highest ever to date.)

John Feigenbaum

1776-1976
Bicentennial Quarter

Mintages & Values

	Mintage	1994 MS65 & PR65 Redbook	CDN
1976	809,784,016	$ .50	$ .35
1976 Proof	3	—	—
1976-D	860,118,839	.50	.35
1976-S Proof clad	7,059,099	1.50	.45
1976-S Silver	11,000,000*	2.25	1.15
1976-S Proof silver	4,000,000*	3.50	1.45

* estimated mintage. See Comments below.

Varieties

101   1976-D. Doubled die obverse. Very rare. An MS60 specimen reportedly sold for $950.[17] (FS#25¢-028, Breen-4452) *(photo)*

Comments

The Bicentennial quarter's history began in 1966 with the establishment of the American Revolution Bicentennial Commission (ARBC). The primary function of this group of congressmen, executive branch members and ordinary citizens was to make recommendations on commemorative coins, medals, stamps and more. In 1973, nearly seven years, dozens of committees and endless reversals of decisions later, it was decided that the quarter, half dollar and dollar reverses would be given a new commemorative design to reflect the celebration. On October 23, the U.S. Treasury announced an open competition for artists. The deadline would be December 14 and all entries were to be in the form of a 10" drawing or photograph of a plaster model. The denominations for the submissions were to be generic (i.e. the selection committee would decide on which coin the design would appear). Ultimately 12 finalists were selected from over 900 entries.

On March 1, 1974, Jack L. Ahr's design was selected as the winner to be used on the quarter. On August 12, Ahr witnessed the first prototypes struck off the press.

The 1976 proof (listed in the the table on the preceding page with a mintage of 3 coins) is a direct result of this prototype minting and thus one of the few modern rarities created by the U.S. Mint. Apparently three special Bicentennial proof sets were produced that day without mintmark for special presentation. Unfortunately none have even been released to the public: one was displayed at the 1974 American Numismatic Convention in Bal Harbour, Florida and is probably retained by the Mint; the second was presented to then-President Ford; the third to his appointment secretary. Perhaps one of the latter two sets will eventually reach collectors' hands.

Bicentennial quarters were released in two different metal alloys. The first being the standard copper-nickel clad for regular circulation and S-mint proofs of the same metal. To make more money from the issue, the San Francisco Mint also produced a 40% silver (with copper-nickel) composition for mintage of proof and non-proof coinage. These were released as late as 1982 until the rising bullion prices of that time rose above selling prices. For this reason the exact quantity distributed is not known, but estimated (see chart on page 135). The West Point branch of the Philadelphia Mint also participated in the production but without a designating mintmark.

Regular-issue mintage of the copper-nickel coins was extremely high in anticipation of tremendous demand by both collectors, hoarders and novelty-seekers alike. Never before or since has the Mint produced a commemorative coin for regular issue. So strong has the hoarding of this coin been that despite a mintage of over 1.6 billion coins it is unusual to find one of these in circulation. Like the $2 bill, wheat cents and other obsolete mint designs, many people believe that these coins will eventually be worth a premium. Unfortunately, the tremendous mintage will prevent this from ever happening.

101. 1976-D Doubled die obverse.
(Photo courtesy of J.T. Stanton – CPG)

1977-Present

Mintages & Values

	Mintage	1994 MS65 & PR65 Redbook	CDN
1977	468,556,000	$ .50	$ .35
1977-D	256,524,978	.50	.35
1977-S Proof	3,251,152	1.50	.55
1978	521,452,000	.50	$ 40
1978-D	287,373,152	.50	.30
1978-S Proof	3,127,781	1.50	.50
1979	515,708,000	.50	$ .40
1979-D	489,789,780	.50	.40
1979-S Pr. Ty.1	3,053,175[18]	1.50	.55
1979-S Pr. Ty.2	624,000[18]	1.75	.60
1980	635,832,000	.50	$ .35
1980-D	518,327,487	.50	.30
1980-S Proof	3,554,806	1.50	.45
1981	601,716,000	.50	$ .30
1981-D	575,722,833	.50	.50
1981-S Proof	4,063,083	1.00	2.40
1982	500,931,000	4.25	$ 3.40
1982-D	480,042,788	2.25	.65
1982-S Proof	3,857,479	1.00	1.50
1983	673,535,000	5.00	$ 4.15
1983-D	617,806,446	7.00	4.50
1983-S Proof	3,279,126	1.25	1.90
1984	676,545,000	.85	$ .55
1984-D	546,483,064	1.75	1.40
1984-S Proof	3,065,110	3.00	1.30
1985	775,818,962	1.25	$ 1.75
1985-D	519,962,888	3.00	2.20
1985-S Proof	3,362,821	2.00	1.05

	Mintage	1994 MS65 & PR65 Redbook	CDN
1986	551,199,333	2.25	$ 3.00
1986-D	504,298,660	2.50	2.15
1986-S Proof	3,010,497	2.50	1.50
1987	582,499,481	.50	$ .35
1987-D	655,594,696	.50	.30
1987-S Proof	4,227,728	1.50	1.00
1988	562,052,000	.50	$ 1.20
1988-D	596,810,688	.50	.35
1988-S Proof	3,262,948	2.25	.35
1989	512,868,000	.50	$ .40
1989-D	896,535,597	.50	.55
1989-S Proof	3,220,194	2.50	.95
1990	613,792,000	.50	$ .35
1990-D	927,638,181	.50	.30
1990-S Proof	3,299,559	2.50	1.75
1991	570,968,000	.50	$ .30
1991-D	630,966,693	.50	.30
1991-S Proof	2,867,787	2.50	2.25
1992	384,764,000	.50	$ .40
1992-D	389,777,107	.50	.30
1992-S Proof	N/A	2.50	2.50
1992-S Pr. Silver	N/A	4.00	4.20
1993	639,276,000[19]	.50	$ .30
1993-D	645,476,128[19]	.50	.30
1993-S Proof	N/A	2.50	2.00
1993-S Pr. Silver	N/A	4.00	4.75

Varieties

101 1977-D. Struck on silver-clad planchet left over from 1976. Breen considers this the "single great rarity" of the 1977-1986 period. (Breen-4457)

102 1977-S Proof. Very thin motto. Result of die overpolishing. Breen estimates that it forms a tiny fraction of all proofs of this year. (Breen-4455)

103 1979-S Proof type 2. Mintmark was replaced due to filling of the old style (type 1). (Breen-4463) *(photo)*

Comments

The Mint resumed the 1974 reverse design and continues to strike these today. The West Point branch of the mint continued making quarters through 1979, however, there is no way to distinguish these from the Philadelphia issues since no mintmark was added. Starting in 1980, the Philadelphia Mint began adding a "P" to their coins in the usual mintmark location.

In 1992 the San Francisco Mint began minting proof specimens in the normal clad and the silver alloys as part of their increased marketing effort to sell more coins.

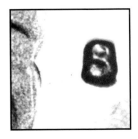

1979-S Proof
Type 1 mintmark

1979-S Proof
Type 2 mintmark

Footnotes

[1] Taxay, Don. *The U.S. Mint and Coinage*. Arco Publishing Co., Inc, p. 361.

[2] Breen, Walter. *Walter Breen's Complete Encyclopedia of U.S. and Colonial Coins*. F.C.I. Press, Inc. & Doubleday, p. 365.

[3] Taxay, Don. p. 362.

[4] Ibid, pp. 362-363.

[5] Ibid, pp. 366.

[6] Pessalano-Filos, Francis. *The Venus Numismatics Dictionary of Artists Engravers, and Die Sinkers*, Eros Publishing Co., pp. 36-37.

[7] *Catalog of Coin Designs and Designers*, pp. 57-58.

[8] Taxay, Don. p. 363.

[9] Breen, Walter. p. 368.

[10] Ibid.

[11] Ibid, p.369.

[12] Ibid.

[13] Ibid.

[14] Ibid.

[15] Ibid, pp. 370-371.

[16] Ibid, p. 370.

[17] Ibid, p. 372.

[18] Herbert, Alan. *Numismatic News*, November 10, 1982, p. 1.

[19] "Endings and Beginnings... Final 1993 Mintages," *Coin World*. February 7, 1994, p. 1.

Appendices

Glossary
•
Statistics
•
References

Appendix A

GLOSSARY

ALTERED COIN - A genuine coin that has been deliberately changed, usually to make it resemble a rare or more valuable piece. For example, by the addition or removal of a mintmark.

ANACS - A coin authentication and grading service located in Columbus, Ohio.

ATTRIBUTION - The identification of a numismatic item by characteristics such as issuing authority, date or period, mint, denomination, metal in which struck and by a standard reference.

BUSINESS STRIKE - A coin which was minted for public circulation. As opposed to a proof.

CHERRYPICKING - The art of searching through a group of coins offered for sale and finding a variety of some value over and above the selling price.

CIRCULATED - Coins showing signs of wear through use in commerce.

COIN DEALER NEWSLETTER (CDN) - A publication reporting current wholesale market values. Published in Torrence, California.

COUNTERFEIT COIN - A coin made outside of the U.S. Mint to imitate a genuine piece with intent to deceive or defraud, irrespective of whether the intended fraud is for monetary or numismatic purposes.

D MINT - Denver Mint.

DDO - Doubled Die Obverse.

DDR - Doubled Die Reverse.

DIE - The metal molds which stamp a design into a blank planchet so the devices and inscriptions will be in relief and readable. The die design is incuse.

DIE CRACK - A raised, usually irregular line on the coin resulting from a crack in one of the dies.

DOUBLED DIE - One which received one of its several blows from a hub or device accidentally punched in imperfect alignment.

FILLED DIE - Results when dirt or grease pack into the letters or numbers preventing the coin metal from entering that part of the design in the dies as the coin is struck.

FLOW LINES - Microscopic striations in a coin's surface caused by the movement of metal under striking pressures.

FROST - Effect caused by striking a coin with sandblasted dies, used in describing some uncirculated and mostly proof coins.

HAIRLINES - Fine scratches in the surface of a coin caused by mishandling or light cleaning. Not to be confused with die scratches or die striations which are raised on the coin.

LUSTER - The sheen or bloom on the surface of an uncirculated numismatic object resulting from the flow of metal caused when struck by the dies.

MASTER DIE - The die made from the master hub in which the year is engraved and used to produce the working hub. The working hubs are then used to produce the working dies utilized by the mint presses.

MINT ERRORS - A coin evidencing a mistake made in its manufacturer at the mint.

MINTMARK - Letter or symbol identifying the mint of origin of a coin. The mint marks are normally punched by hand into each working die at the Philadelphia Mint.

NGC - Numismatic Guaranty Corporation of America. A coin certification and grading service located in Parsippany, New Jersey.

OBVERSE - The "heads" side of a coin. The side with the date.

OVERDATE- A variety in which at least one digit of a date has been changed either for mint economy or to correct a blunder. Some part of the earlier date still shows.

P MINT - Philadelphia Mint.

PCGS - Professional Coin Grading Service. An independent certification and grading service located in Newport Beach, California.

PLANCHET - The blank disc of metal on which the dies of the coins are impressed to make the coin. Also called a blank or disc.

PROOF - Specially minted coin, normally given two or more blows from the dies to bring up the designs more sharply than on production coins. Usually minted on burnished blanks from burnished dies giving the coins a mirror finish.

RED BOOK - *"A GUIDE BOOK OF THE UNITED STATES COINS"* by R.S. Yeoman, published by Western Publishing Company, Inc., of Racine, Wisconsin. A retail price guide.

REVERSE - The "tails" side of a coin. In this series, the side with the eagle.

RPM - Repunched Mintmark. The mintmark has been punched into the die twice resulting in a doubled mintmark on the coin. Since the doubling appears on the die itself, identical specimens are produced and the variety is considered collectable.

S MINT San Francisco Mint.

SLAB - A coin encased in hard plastic by one of the certification services. After grading, the enclosed coins receive protection from the outside environment. The holders are tamper resistant.

SLIDER - Current slang for a coin that is close to uncirculated (AU58) and possibly saleable as mint state, particularly after cleaning and/or recoloring.

STRIKE -The quality of the coin's detail transferred from the dies. Poor strikes can be caused by light striking pressure, worn dies or improper distant adjustments between the obverse and reverse dies.

WHIZZING - The severe polishing or buffing of a coin in an attempt to improve its appearance and salability to the uninformed. A form of alteration regarded as misleading by the numismatic community and which actually lowers the value of the coin significantly.

VARIETY - Any coin which is recognizably different from another of the same design, type, date and mint due to a difference in the die which produced it.

Appendix B

STATISTICS

Table 1. The rank of Washington quarter business strikes by mintage, from lowest to highest.

Date	Quantity Minted	Date	Quantity Minted
1932-S	408,000	1941-S	16,080,000
1932-D	436,800	1943-D	16,095,600
1937-S	1,652,000	1941-D	16,714,800
1939-S	2,628,000	1948-D	16,766,800
1940-D	2,797,600	1945-S	17,004,001
1938-S	2,832,000	1942-D	17,487,200
1955-D	3,182,400	1955	18,180,181
1934-D	3,527,200	1953	18,536,120
1936-S	3,828,000	1942-S	19,384,000
1946-S	4,204,000	1937	19,696,000
1936-D	5,374,000	1950-D	21,075,600
1932	5,404,000	1943-S	21,700,000
1947-S	5,532,000	1947	22,556,000
1935-S	5,660,000	1959	24,384,000
1935-D	5,780,000	1950	24,920,126
1958	6,360,000	1960	29,164,000
1939-D	7,092,000	1934	31,912,052
1937-D	7,189,600	1956-D	32,334,500
1940-S	8,244,000	1935	32,484,000
1951-S	9,048,000	1939	33,540,000
1946-D	9,072,800	1948	35,196,000
1949	9,312,000	1951-D	35,354,800
1938	9,472,000	1940	35,704,0000
1949-D	10,068,400	1962	36,156,000
1950-S	10,284,004	1961	37,036,000
1976-S*	11,000,000	1952	38,780,093
1954-S	11,834,722	1936	41,300,000
1945-D	12,341,600	1954-D	42,305,500
1944-S	12,560,000	1951	43,448,102
1952-S	13,707,800	1956	44,144,000
1953-S	14,016,000	1957	46,532,000
1944-D	14,600,800	1952-D	49,795,200
1947-D	15,338,400	1946	53,436,000
1948-S	15,960,000	1954	54,412,203

John Feigenbaum

Table 1. *Continued*

Date	Quantity Minted	Date	Quantity Minted
1953-D	56,112,400	1986-D	504,298,660
1959-D	62,054,232	1989	512,868,000
1960-D	63,000,324	1979	515,708,000
1963	74,316,000	1980-D	518,327,487
1945	74,372,000	1985-D	519,962,888
1957-D	77,924,160	1978	521,452,000
1958-D	78,124,900	1984-D	546,483,064
1941	79,032,000	1986	551,199,333
1961-D	83,656,928	1964	560,390,585
1943	99,700,000	1988	562,052,000
1968-D	101,534,000	1991	570,968,000
1942	101,996,000	1981-D	575,722,833
1944	104,956,000	1987	582,499,481
1971	109,284,000	1988-D	596,810,688
1969-D	114,372,000	1981	601,716,000
1962-D	127,554,756	1990	613,792,000
1963-D	135,288,184	1983-D	617,806,446
1970	136,420,000	1991-D	630,966,693
1969	176,212,000	1980	635,832,000
1972	215,048,000	1993	639,276,000
1968	220,731,500	1993-D	645,476,128
1973-D	232,977,400	1987-D	655,594,696
1977-D	256,524,978	1983	673,535,000
1971-D	258,634,428	1984	676,545,000
1978-D	287,373,152	1964-D	704,135,528
1972-D	311,067,732	1985	775,818,962
1973	346,924,000	1974	801,456,000
1974-D	353,160,300	1976	809,784,016
1992	384,764,000	1966	821,101,500
1992-D	389,777,107	1976-D	860,118,839
1970-D	417,341,364	1989-D	896,535,597
1977	468,556,000	1990-D	927,638,181
1982-D	480,042,788	1967	1,524,031,848
1979-D	489,789,780	1965	1,819,717,540
1982	500,931,000		

Table 2. The rank of Washington quarter business strikes by total yearly mintage, from lowest to highest.

Year	Quantity Minted	Year	Quantity Minted	Year	Quantity Minted
1932	6,248,800	1952	102,283,093	1966	821,101,500
1938	12,304,000	1945	103,717,601	1982	980,973,788
1949	19,380,400	1954	108,552,425	1979	1,005,497,780
1955	21,362,581	1941	111,826,800	1986	1,055,497,993
1937	28,537,600	1961	120,692,928	1980	1,154,159,487
1934	35,439,252	1957	124,456,160	1974	1,154,616,300
1939	43,260,000	1944	132,116,800	1988	1,158,862,688
1947	43,426,400	1943	137,495,600	1981	1,177,438,833
1935	43,924,000	1942	138,867,200	1991	1,201,934,693
1940	46,745,600	1962	163,710,756	1984	1,223,028,064
1936	50,502,000	1963	209,604,184	1987	1,238,094,177
1950	56,279,730	1969	290,584,000	1964	1,264,526,113
1946	66,712,800	1968	322,265,500	1993	1,284,752,128
1948	67,922,800	1971	367,918,428	1983	1,291,341,446
1956	76,478,500	1972	526,115,732	1985	1,295,781,850
1958	84,484,900	1970	553,761,364	1989	1,409,403,597
1959	86,438,232	1973	579,901,400	1967	1,524,031,848
1951	87,850,902	1977	725,080,978	1990	1,541,430,181
1953	88,664,520	1992	774,541,107	1976	1,680,902,855
1960	92,164,324	1978	808,825,152	1965	1,822,077,540

Table 3. The mintage of proof Washington quarters by year.

Year	Proofs Minted	Year	Proofs Minted
1936	3,837	1970	2,632,810
1937	5,542	1971	3,220,733
1938	8,045	1972	3,260,996
1939	8,795	1973	2,760,339
1940	11,246	1974	2,612,568
1941	15,287	1976 (clad)	7,059,099
1942	21,123	1976 (silver)	4,000,000
1950	51,386	1977	3,251,152
1951	57,500	1978	3,127,781
1952	81,980	1979	3,677,175
1953	128,800	1980	3,554,806
1954	233,300	1981	4,063,083
1955	378,200	1982	3,857,479
1956	669,384	1983	3,279,126
1957	1,247,952	1984	3,065,110
1958	875,652	1985	3,362,821
1959	1,149,291	1986	3,010,497
1960	1,691,602	1987	4,227,728
1961	3,028,244	1988	3,262,948
1962	3,218,019	1989	3,220,194
1963	3,075,645	1990	3,299,559
1964	3,950,762	1991	2,867,787
1968	3,041,506	1992	N/A
1969	2,934,631		

John Feigenbaum

Appendix C

REFERENCES

Breen, Walter. *Walter Breen's Complete Encyclopedia of U.S. and Colonial Coins*. F.C.I. Press, Inc. & Doubleday. New York, 1988.

Doyle, Al. "Why Not Washington Quarters?," *Coins*. August 1991, pp.46-48.

"Endings and Beginnings... Final 1993 Mintages," *Coin World*. February 7, 1994, p. 1.

Fivaz, Bill & Stanton, J.T. *The Cherrypickers' Guide to Rare Die Varieties*, Second Edition. Published by the authors. Savannah, GA, 1991.

Ganz, David L. "Tribute to 200 Years of Freedom: The Story of How the United States Got Its Bicentennial Coinage," *The Numismatist*. March-June 1975, pp. 499-519, 761-776, 1010-1029, 1239-1249.

Hicks, Herbert P. "The Washington Quarter Reverse: A Die Variety Bonanza," *The Numismatist*. February 1986, pp. 244-261.

Pessalano-Filos, Francis. *The Venus Numismatics Dictionary of Artists, Engravers, and Die Sinkers*. Eros Publishing Co., New York, pp.36-37.

Spadone, F.G. *Major Variety – Oddity Guide of United States Coins*, 7th Edition. Published by the author. 1977.

Taxay, Don. *The U.S. Mint and Coinage*. Arco Publishing Co., Inc, New York, 1966.

United States Treasury Department. *Annual Report of the Director of the Mint for the Fiscal Year Ended June 30, 1932*. U.S. Government Printing Office, Washington D.C., 1932.

United States Department of the Treasury. *Annual Report of the Director of the Mint: Fiscal Year Ended June 30, 1976 and Transition Quarter*. U.S. Government Printing Office, Washington D.C., 1976.

Wexler, John A. & Miller, Tom. *The RPM Book*. Lonesome John Publishing Co., Newbury Park, CA, 1983.

Yeoman, R.S. *A Guide Book of United States Coins*. Western Publishing Co., Inc., Racine, WI, 1949, 1964, 1979, 1989, 1991, 1994.

ABOUT THE AUTHOR

John Feigenbaum is a senior numismatist at David Lawrence Rare Coins. A graduate of Virginia Tech, John has been a familiar face on the coin show circuit since 1979 when he helped his father set up at small shows in the South Florida area. While this is his first book, John has been instrumental in the publication of 11 other numismatic titles ranging from Brigg's book on Seated quarters to the Van Allen/Mallis Encyclopedia of Morgan and Peace Dollars.

Application for Membership in the American Numismatic Association

Check One:
- ❏ Regular ❏ Junior ❏ Associate ❏ Senior
- ❏ 3-Year ❏ 5-Year ❏ Life ❏ Club

Present or former ANA No., if any _____

❏ Mr. ❏ Mrs. ❏ Ms. ❏ Club

Name (please print) _____

Street _____

City _____ State _____ Zip _____

Birthdate _____

ANA Bylaws require the publication of each applicant's name & state.

❏ Check here if you DO NOT want your name and address forwarded to the ANA club representative in your area.

❏ Check here if you would like your name provided to companies with numismatic offers we feel may interest you.

I herewith make application for membership in the American Numismatic Association, subject to the bylaws of said Association. I also agree to abide by the Code of Ethics adopted by the Association.

_____
Signature of applicant   Date

_____
Signature of Parent or Guardian (for Jr. applicant)
❏ Check ❏ VISA ❏ MasterCard ❏ Am Ex

_____
Credit Card Account No. (all digits)

_____
Signature of Cardholder (required)

DUES:
Regular Member (adult)* $26
Senior Member (age 65+)* .. $22
Regular Foreign Member* ... $28
Club Membership* $30
Junior (age 17 or less) $11
Associate (child or spouse of ANA member living at same address) $4
3-Year Member $70
5-Year Member $115
Life Member (Individual) $750**
Senior Life Member (age 65+) $500**
Life Membership (Club) .. $1,250

* *First year, add processing fee of $6*
** *Payment plan available*

Please photocopy this page to use as your application.